"I AM"
The Key to Mastery

by
Peter Mt. Shasta

Published by
Church of the Seven Rays
PO Box 711
Mount Shasta, CA 96067 USA

Copyright 2022, by Peter Mt. Shasta

ISBN: 979-8415976294

All rights reserved. No part of this book may be reproduced, stored in a retrieval system, or transmitted by any means without the written permission of the author.

For more information:
www.I-AM-Teachings.com

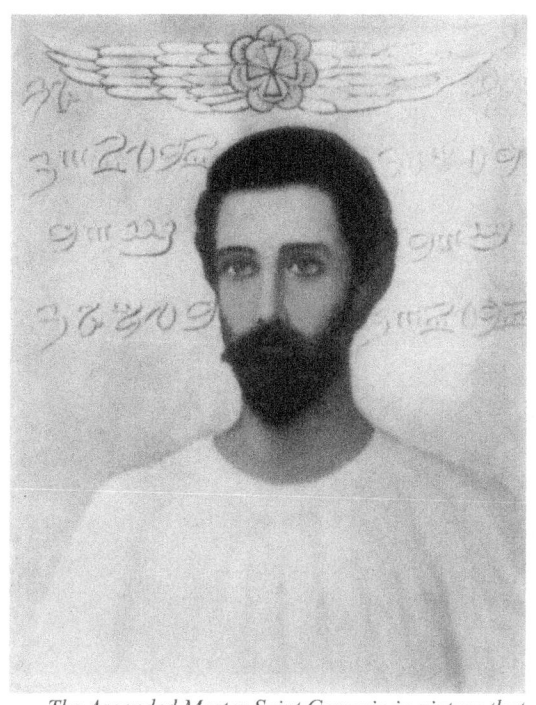

The Ascended Master Saint Germain in picture that he precipitated for Godfre Ray King.

How this Book Originated

This was originally a collection of transcripts of talks that I gave online over a decade. To make them available in book format, I tried to delete colloquial expressions and eliminate repetition to make the book more readable. Thus, the text is less formally organized than if it had been written as a book from start to finish according to a plan. That is its nature.

Note of Gratitude

I would like to thank, Kevin Barnett, Victoria Bowen, Christine and Thomas Carlisle, Juno Dawson, Annika Sophia Grace, Matt O'Connell, and Amanda and Jordan Sunshine, for their invaluable assistance in the editing of this book.

Who are you?
-Neem Karoli Baba to Peter Mt. Shasta, Naini Tal, India, 1971

Meditate on I AM.
-Sathya Sai Baba to Peter Mt. Shasta Puttaparthi, India, 1972

You are That.
(Sanskrit: *Tat Twam Asi*)
-Vedas[1]

I Am God.
(Sanskrit: *Aham Brahmasmi*)

---

[1] The *Vedas* are oral teachings of the *rishis,* enlightened beings who, after the destruction of the previous civilization *(Pralaya),* give spiritual guidance at the beginning of every new age. Scholars believe some of them to have been given orally prior to 7,000 BCE, but not put in writing until 2,000 to 200 BCE.

Vedas

As pure water poured into pure water becomes one, so also is it with the Self of an illumined Knower.
—Katha Upanishad

The Self is subtler than the subtle, greater than the great; It dwells in the heart of each living being. He who is free from desire and free from grief, with mind and senses tranquil, beholds the glory of the God Self (Atman).
—Katha Upanishad

The highest meditation is on the Tejobindu (Jyoti), the point of light of the Self, abiding in the heart, the provider of joy and peace, that which transcends all.
-Tejobindu Upanishad

I AM Consciousness....I AM nondual, pure in form, absolute knowledge, absolute love....I AM the Atman (I AM Presence), that reveals itself as Satchidananda, pure being, consciousness and bliss.
-Tejobindu Upanishad

Table of Contents

CHAPTER 1 9
   Am I Enlightened? 9

CHAPTER 2 15
   Eastern Spirituality Comes West 15

CHAPTER 3 25
   Origin of "I AM" 25

CHAPTER 4 35
   Contacting the Presence 35

CHAPTER 5 43
   The I AM Presence Returns 43

CHAPTER 6 51
   Getting Rid of Karma 51

CHAPTER 7 55
   Be God in Action 55

CHAPTER 8 67
   What is the Name of God? 67

CHAPTER 9 81
   What Is the Self? 81

CHAPTER 10 97

Advice for Difficult Times	97
CHAPTER 11	**107**
Meditation in Action at a Cafe	107
CHAPTER 12	**111**
Meditation on Consciousness	111
CHAPTER 13	**123**
The Pearl of Great Price	123
Pearl's Open-Eyed Meditation	127
CHAPTER 14	**133**
Your Power to Create	133
CHAPTER 15	**141**
What About the World?	141
CHAPTER 16	**145**
Other Meditations	145
CHAPTER 17	**147**
Methods of Meditation	147
CHAPTER 18	**169**
Concise Method of Liberation	169
Afterword	177
Other Books by Peter Mt. Shasta	185

Chapter 1
Am I Enlightened?

There is an old saying:

*Those who know, do not say,
those who say, do not know.*

While that is not true in all circumstances, there is much truth to the statement. Many people consider themselves enlightened, and they are so convinced of it that they cannot stop talking about it. In fact, many of these self-proclaimed Buddhas talk incessantly. Is that really enlightenment?

Many people have an experience of God Consciousness but are still attached to their ego with all its unresolved desires and emotional attachments. Yet, they cling to their transitory experiences of expanded awareness, believing they are fully enlightened. It is not that simple.

What is enlightenment? Literally, it is to be filled with Light. However, if you were totally filled with Light in every cell of your being, you would dematerialize and attain what, in Tibet, is called the Rainbow Body *(jalus),* and in English, ascension. Matter is an illusion, as Einstein said, everything being simply energy, vibration, and thought. When you know that in every fiber of your being, in every aspect of conscious awareness, you are Master over the world of illusion—and there is certainly no desire to discuss it. This is why most of the truly enlightened beings throughout history have preferred silence. After attaining enlightenment, Buddha was going to wander off and remain unknown until the God Brahma appeared and asked him to teach others.[2]

Ramana Maharshi, a yogi who attained enlightenment on Mount Arunachala in Southern India, remained in silence, communicating only occasionally via a

---

[2] Very little is actually known about the real life of the one known as the Buddha.

blackboard. Even then, what he did say when asked a question was often: *Who is it that is asking?* He did not go on and on about his spiritual experiences, trying to attract followers.

The amazing yogis I met in India, some of whom were Masters, did not talk at all. Neem Karoli Baba Maharajji, the guru of Ram Dass and many other Americans, talked very little, his main instruction being *Love people and feed them.*

Why don't most enlightened people talk? Because there is almost nothing to say about the experience of total Emptiness (Sanskrit: *shunyata*) that is characteristic of the enlightened state. The one thing that Maharajji and other great yogis have said about enlightenment from the beginning of time is: *Sub Ek*, Sanskrit for All is One.

This does not mean, however, that something about the path to enlightenment cannot be taught. There are many paths, some being more appropriate than others, depending on where the individual is on the path of awakening. For me, it was hatha yoga that initiated me on my path of awakening, leading to formal meditation on the breath, self-inquiry into the nature of the Self, contemplation of the Inner Light, meditation on the *I That I AM,* and so forth.

One of my greatest moments of awakening happened while shoveling horse manure, when I spontaneously experienced *Satchidananda*—Being, Consciousness, and Bliss, free of all sense of self. But I can hardly offer that as a path. For some people, becoming a parent may be their path to that same state of selfless Awareness.

I would say to those who feel they are enlightened, observe who it is that feels it has reached the end of the path, and who is it that feels the need to express that to others?

Who is enlightened?
Who is observing the enlightenment?
Who wants to talk about it?

This process of self-observation will eventually take you to the Real Self, the One About Whom Nothing May Be Said.

Nothing can be said about it because *it* is beyond words. A true teacher can only point in the right direction, but it is you who has to go in that direction and follow the path.

What is more, and shocking to some, is that enlightenment is not the end of the path. There are many yogis who achieved enlightenment in a past life and then returned to embody again on Earth. Why? Because they had not developed compassion for others nor attained Mastery. They were only concerned with their own awakening, liberation, and bliss—not the liberation of their fellow sufferers. If you are advanced on the path, you will feel the suffering of humanity, and want to alleviate the causes of that suffering. This compassion is where the path of Mastery begins.

Chapter 2
Eastern Spirituality Comes West

The teachings on finding the inner God Self were given under the inspiration and guidance of one known as Saint Germain. *The man who knows everything and never dies,* is how he was described by the French philosopher and writer Voltaire. As a Master who has raised his physical body into one of Light, he gave a series of teachings in the 1930s through Guy Ballard (pen name: Godfre Ray King), giving instructions on how the individual can find God within. He further instructed how to call that God Presence forth to bring about manifestation of one's thoughts through the use of the words *I AM.* Whatever thoughts, feelings and words follow *I AM* determine what you bring into being. These keys to Mastery were given as part of the consciousness of self-empowerment that the Masters began to transmit to humanity at that time. Prior to that, the Judeo-Christian tradition dominated Western religious thought.[3] These initial keys were only the first in the initiation of the West into long-hidden spiritual teachings from the Far East.

Buddhism and Taoism were introduced to the United States by Chinese immigrants in the mid eighteen-hundreds. With the founding of the Theosophical Society in 1875 by Helena Petrovna Blavatsky, the new age of self-knowledge and spiritual empowerment began. Through this society, the Ascended Masters El Morya, Kuthumi, Saint Germain, and others, began to release to the public the Eastern spiritual teachings that had long been held secret or only discussed in occult groups.

---

[3] The teachings on the use of "I AM" are hidden in the words of Jesus in the New Testament, affirmations such as: *I AM the Light that lighteth everyone who comes into the World.* This aspect of Jesus's teachings can be seen in *"I AM" the Living Christ, Teachings of Jesus,* by Peter Mt. Shasta (Church of the Seven Rays, 2017).

In 1893, Eastern teachings were further introduced in the West by Swami Vivekananda at the Parliament of World's Religions in Chicago. He quoted the *Shiva Mahimna Stotram:*

As the different streams having their sources in different places all mingle their water in the sea, so, O Lord, the different paths which men take through different tendencies, various though they appear...all lead to Thee. Whosoever comes to Me, through whatsoever form, I reach him; all men are struggling through paths that in the end lead to Me (God).

Another major spiritual infusion occurred in 1920 when Paramahansa Yogananda visited the United States. He soon founded the Self-Realization Fellowship, which spread the teachings of yoga and *Vedanta.*[4] Because his book,

---

[4] Vedanta is the wisdom revealed to sages in ancient India, later recorded in texts known as the Vedas.

Autobiography of a Yogi, fascinated so many people with its phenomenal tales of the mystics of India, interest in Eastern teachings became widespread.

There were many other highly advanced beings who revealed spiritual teachings as a part of the general awakening of consciousness in the West, among them: Rudolf Steiner, George Gurdjieff, Peter Ouspensky, Alexandra David-Néel, Omraam Mikhaël Aïvanhov, and the Dalai Lama.

Other teachers who brought the ancient wisdom to the West were Alice Bailey, Annie Besant, William Quan Judge, Jiddu Krishnamurti, Shunryu Suzuki, Alan Watts, and Chögyam Trungpa Rinpoche.

Krishnamurti was raised by the Theosophists to be the new World Teacher, a Christ, but he declined to fill

---

The underlying teaching is to inquire within yourself, *What is that which, by being known, everything else becomes known?*

that role. Instead, he encouraged his followers to find the truth within themselves—helping turn people away from slavish worship of gurus and to instead engage in self-inquiry.

In the 1930s and for the next few decades, positive statements known as I AM affirmations were repeated verbally but mainly using will and mental force rather than spiritual consciousness. Even though Saint Germain gave meditation instruction in the first chapter of *Unveiled Mysteries*, few practiced the method. Now people have realized that when an affirmation is said from a higher consciousness, containing love from the Source, a greater power is invoked. That connection with the Source is only attainable through stilling the mind and purifying the emotions, which happens in meditation through self-observation. Only then can the individual begin to manifest Mastery in everyday life.

This flow of Eastern mysticism continued in 1961, with the arrival to the United States of Maharishi Mahesh Yogi. After the Beatles visited him in India, his Transcendental Meditation became widely practiced, and the words "guru," "meditation," "nirvana," and "enlightenment" soon entered mainstream conversation. Hatha Yoga gradually became popular, especially after the saintly looking Swami Satchidananda gave the opening prayer at the Woodstock Music Festival with the words:

America is helping everybody in the material field, but the time has come for America to help the whole world with spirituality also.

Former Harvard psychology professor Richard Alpert, later known as Ram Dass, also initiated a mass awakening of America's youth. He had experimented with the clinical use of psilocybin to alleviate neuroses. In 1967, in search of a way to attain through natural means the spiritual insights that many were experiencing through LSD and plant entheogens (substances that produce an awareness of *Theo*: God), he went to

India. His story of transformation through finding his guru, Neem Karoli Baba, became an inspiration for an entire generation of American youth. His book *Be Here Now*,[5] published by the Lama Foundation in 1971, became an instant best-seller as it spoke directly to the younger generation who were practicing meditation and awakening to the existence of alternate realities and higher states of consciousness.

When the Communist Chinese invaded Tibet in 1950, many highly realized lamas fled the country, bringing Tibetan Buddhism with them. This fulfilled the prophecy of Padmasambhava made 1250 years before: *When the iron bird flies and horses run on wheels, the Tibetan people will be scattered like ants over the face of the earth, and the Dharma will go to the land of the Red Man.*[6] Tibetan Buddhism

---

[5] *Be Here Now*, by Ram Dass (Harmony, 1971)

[6] To prevent their destruction, Guru Rinpoche concealed countless teachings, not

began to be widely studied and practiced in America. One of the foremost of these teachers was the Tibetan lama, Chögyam Trungpa Rinpoche. He studied at Oxford University and married an English woman, so was eminently able to converse fluently with the hippie generation— while at the same time imparting advanced spiritual concepts. He initiated the founding of many meditation centers around the world and made the techniques of Buddhist mind training available in English, free of religious terminology, dogma, and the trappings of Tibetan culture.

In the context of this Western expansion of consciousness, Saint Germain has been prompting me to further expand Western spirituality by the incorporation of the ancient wisdom and spiritual practices of the Far East. His

---

only in physical locations, but also transmitted them to the minds of certain of his followers— to be revealed in the future, which is now.

introduction of the I AM in the 1930s was not meant to be the final word on spirituality, but a prelude to what was to follow. More advanced teachings on Mastery are here given to those whose minds are open and receptive.

Chapter 3
Origin of "I AM"

In the Vedic teachings of India, which come from enlightened beings, it is stated that before the consciousness of *I AM* was the consciousness of *I*, the Supreme Self that is the origin of all things. Prior to the awareness of that *I,* was Pure Being, the consciousness of which is experienced as *satchidananda*, a Sanskrit word meaning truth, consciousness, and bliss.

This state of pure being is said to last for a great cycle of time called a *kalpa,* approximately 4.32 billion earth years. Then another kalpa of Creation begins again. These cycles of oneness and duality are like days and nights of God. As God awakens to a new day and becomes self-aware, that awareness manifests as the sound of the cosmic *OM* (Sanskrit: *pranava)*. The Supreme Self awakens to the sense of Self, the eternal *I*. From that *I* the seven rays emerge—the seven aspects of consciousness, which manifest visibly on Earth as the colors of the rainbow. These seven aspects take the form of seven cosmic Masters, the *Saptarishis* (Hebrew: *Elohim*). As God (Sanskrit: *Brahman)* awakens fully, the Supreme Consciousness can then say *I AM.* This is the Word that creates all that is. *I* is awareness of Self—*AM* is the expression of the creative urge, expressing the dual nature of God as both father and mother. Thus, from the Source, where there is no ego, evolves the awareness of Self, which is then followed by the awareness of other. Even in that initial consciousness, the other is still realized to be an emanation of Self. In other words, as one of the great sayings of the Vedas says: *Tat Twam Asi:* You are that! (All that is, you are.)

Saint Germain encourages us to meditate on this same truth in the affirmation:

I AM here, I AM there, I AM everywhere.

As Source Consciousness takes form in increasingly numerous and dense forms, the original consciousness of Self as God disappears—and Oneness begins to identify with the illusory self. In the *Bhagavad Gita,* the avatar of God known as Krishna tries to awaken the prince, Arjuna, to the omnipresence of God, saying:

I AM in the flower...as well as the twinkling star....I AM the Self, seated in the heart of all beings! I AM the beginning, middle, and also the end of all beings....I AM the Source of all; from Me everything evolves. Understanding this, the wise man meditates on Me.

The I AM statements attributed to Jesus in the New Testament were ancient truths that Jesus learned on his extensive travels in India, but which were only written in a book hundreds of years later when Emperor Constantine ordered the creation of the Bible. In the *Book of Exodus*, when Moses asks God what to call Him, God is reported to have said: *Ayeh Asher Ayeh.* This has been incorrectly translated in the modern Bible as *I am that I am*. In Hebrew, the language in which this was first written, the meaning is *I will be what I will be*. In other words, *I will respond to any name, appear in whatever form, by which I am invoked.* That is a teaching of *tantra* (unbroken awareness), that you can invoke God by any name, any form, and so merge with that Deity to experience Divine Consciousness. In so doing you regain awareness of yourself as a God. In practicing tantra, you merge with your chosen form of God and so regain your innate Cosmic Awareness.[7]

This realization was transmitted by Joseph Benner in his 1914 book, *The Impersonal Life.* Here is likely where Guy Ballard first became acquainted with what he later called the I AM Teachings. He also studied Theosophy and was friends with Baird T. Spalding, author of *The Life*

---

[7] For more on tantra, as well as how to invoke the Violet Fire, see both my books: *I AM the Violet Tara* and *I AM Violet Tara in Action* (Church of the Seven Rays).

and Teachings of the Masters of the Far East, which talks of the Ascended Masters and their teachings.

Many current students of Buddhism are shocked when a lama says, *You must destroy the sense of "I."* What the lama means is that one needs to destroy identification with the ego as the Self. In the tantric teachings of Buddhism, you will still find the expression *I am* (followed by the name of whatever God is being invoked). The Deity is a mirror of an aspect of your True Self—the I AM Presence.

Oneness is not only our origin but the destination to which we will someday return. Connection with the consciousness of our True Selves is necessary for I AM affirmations to be truly effective. Without this connection, without this love for the Source, affirmations are simply words empowered by the will of the ego trying to force the changes it desires—without regard for the Divine Plan held by the God Self. The teachings from the 1930's did not put much emphasis on the need for meditation, introspection, and self-examination, hoping that one's negative tendencies could be eliminated through the use of verbal affirmations alone. These negative tendencies, embodied as self-created thought forms, become the Dweller at the Threshold, an entity that follows a person from lifetime to lifetime until it is dissolved through conscious self-examination and invocation of Violet Fire.[8] This Dweller tries to influence human action and derives its sustenance from the negative emotions produced.[9]

---

[8] Violet Fire is the most purifying quality of Light, which is invoked in meditation through an outpouring of love to the God Self while at the same time visualizing dazzling Violet Light. This etheric fire dissolves negative energy and transmutes and purifies all that it touches. It is a natural quality of consciousness, the teachings of which were revealed to humanity in the 1930s by Saint Germain through Godfre Ray King.

[9] The Dweller at the Threshold is a Western term also used by Rudolf Steiner, who described it as an astral entity. It is composed of energies called in Sanskrit, *Vrittis* or *Kleshas*—the source

These habitual thought and energy patterns of the Dweller can only be cleared through self-observation, invocation of the Light of Consciousness, and especially active, dynamic, and consistent use of the Violet Consuming Fire. Only then, when one ceases to identify with the false self that is the cause of suffering, does one achieve liberation and break the cycle of endless re-embodiment.

The I AM Presence, the God Self that resides above every person, can be contacted at every moment within the heart center, where it is anchored. That Presence is the power that sustains and animates us, and from which we are never separate. To hear God's response to our thoughts it is necessary to first still the

---

of the conflicting emotions and voices that sometimes arise when one tries to still the mind. It is an actual presence that follows one from life to life like an alternate personality until it is confronted and consciously dissolved. The Dweller features prominently in the 1842 book *Zanoni,* by Edward Bulwer-Lytton.

mind. This happens through turning the attention inward to the Unfed Flame (known in Sanskrit as the *jyoti* or *tejobindu)*.

To purify the lower self, that self must first be observed. Through meditation, one is able to observe and dissolve the illusions of the ego and free oneself of the unconscious motivations that bring one back lifetime after lifetime. Self-observation and meditation must be incorporated into daily life in order to achieve Mastery. It is in relationship with others that those illusions needing dissolution emerge and can be more easily seen.

A Simple Meditation[10]

A basic yet powerful way to meditate is first to attain tranquility (Pali*: shamatha)*. This sense of peace can be attained by simply observing one's breathing. Turn

---

[10] This method is given again in slightly different format under "Vipassana" on p.147.

your attention inward and feel the inbreath and outbreath, and the procession of thoughts begins to slow. Label these thoughts simply as "thought," and allow them to dissolve. Then return your attention to the breath. Gradually, your mind dwells between the thoughts—in a state of emptiness. Allow your mind to expand outward into space and merge with unconditional awareness. The awareness of a personal self dissolves into pure being. Although, at first, it may seem as if nothing is happening, after a while, moments of transcendent awareness arise and increase in depth and duration.

The second step in this meditation is self-inquiry, known in Sanskrit as *Vipassana*. Having first attained a sense of calmness, one asks inwardly *Who am I?* More precisely, *Who is the observer?* Or rather, *What is the Observer?* This furthers the transfer of attention from the human self to the Divine Self. Observe the attachment to repetitive thought patterns and follow them to their source—where they dissolve.

To have dominion over the world, we first need to have dominion over ourselves. For there to be world peace, we need first to achieve inner peace. For there to be love, we first need to have Self-Love. By Self-Love I do not mean love of the ego or personality, but love of the True Self, the focus of which can be felt in the focus we call the Heart, the *Jyoti*, beneath the sternum. This is an expanded path to Mastery for those who desire to benefit others.

Chapter 4
Contacting the Presence
From a talk on February 27, 2021

Saint Germain's core teaching is that God is your Higher Self—the I AM Presence. Secondly, he teaches how to call that God Presence into action with the words *I AM.* Not only are you an outer expression of the I AM Presence, but that consciousness exists in all that is.

When I saw this Presence on two occasions I was in awe. I described both encounters in the second part of my autobiography, *Apprentice to the Masters.* In both cases I was awakened from sleep to behold the all-powerful Presence above me, after which It began to speak. After the first encounter there was no doubt in my mind that the I AM Presence was more than an artistic painting of a Theosophical concept. Since then, I have felt I have a duty to convey the reality of this Presence.

I would now like to help you contact your own I AM Presence so you can invite It more fully into your life. You can then converse with and become One with the God Source. In doing so you become of immense benefit to all beings. This truth has been known throughout time in almost every culture.

In India, this Presence is known as the *Atman*, in Tibetan Buddhism, the *Dharmakaya* (the body of Dharma). The Tibetans call the middle body (Higher Mental Body or Christ Self) the *Sambhogakaya*, while the physical body is the *Nirmanakaya*. Initiates have always known this. It has been the work of Saint Germain to make the reality of this I AM Presence and the various subtle bodies known to humanity—so that each can be aware that they are an embodiment of God.

The question arises, of course, *If I am a God why do I seem to have so many limitations?*

That is because our attention is continually drawn to outer objects, conditions, thoughts, and emotions, which keep us from seeing that unlimited Self. In meditation we return our attention to Source and the limitations drop away.

The original painting of the I AM Presence came about through May De Camara, a woman who was in the audience at one of the discourses of Godfre Ray King. After the discourse was over, she came up to him and said words to the effect, "I saw this amazing ball of light emanating rainbow colors above you. Then I saw another body, a light body, over your physical body. Godfre said, "Can you paint this?"

She said, "I will try."

This is the painting now used by the Saint Germain Foundation to depict the Higher Self that resides above the human self.[11] Godfre Ray King said that this

---

[11] The I AM Presence has also been portrayed in Tibetan thangkas (wall hangings), showing the Presence as Amitabha Buddha (Lord of Infinite Light) at the top, the Christ Self as Chenrezig (Lord of Compassion) in the middle, and the human self as a particular physical being, usually Padmasambhava, at the bottom of the thangka. Other Western artists

image was so important that a copy should be in everyone's home throughout the world.

Saint Germain wanted me to talk about this because it is the essence of his work and our work too. We should not get so absorbed in what is happening in our lives or in the news that we forget the Source. In that Source is our freedom. *Our freedom from all limitation is in the I AM Presence.*

When Saint Germain sent me to Mount Shasta to study with Pearl, now an Ascended Master, I saw the picture of the I AM Presence, but I took its reality with a grain of salt. I thought, "Well, you know artists; they have good imaginations, and this is just an artist's interpretation of your Higher Self."

As I continued studying with Pearl, I would wake up at night and see various Ascended Masters standing beside my bed

---

have painted other versions, such as the original one by Marius Michael-George and another by Amoraea, showing the lower figure as a woman.

conveying teachings. Frequently, in the morning I would not remember consciously what they had said, but it was very clear that this was not a dream. After a while I started to hear a new voice that I didn't recognize. After the second night this happened, I woke in the morning, and said, "I want to know who you are, so if you come to me again I would like you to introduce yourself and tell me your name."

That night I was awakened by a dazzling light near the ceiling. It was like the painting of the I AM Presence in *Unveiled Mysteries*, except brighter than the sun. It was dazzling. Wide awake, I shouted, "Who are you?"

It replied:

I am you! I am your own God Presence!

With that, I passed out. I awakened the next morning with the vivid memory of what had happened. This was not a dream. I had been sitting up wide awake in bed.

Then I knew the reality of the I AM Presence. So, it is not true that no one has ever seen God. Pearl could not only see her I AM Presence, but she could also converse with It.

Sometimes the student gets an opportunity to return energy to the teacher. One day, Pearl was not feeling well. At that time, she was living in Yreka, and I was in Mount Shasta. I visualized that I was standing by her bed, and I said: *I AM the Presence of God blessing Pearl.* Then I stood up, as though beside her bed, and held my hands up, imagining the Light going down into her.

Then I said:

I AM the Healing Presence of God in action.

The next day, although I didn't tell her anything, she asked, "What were you doing at this time yesterday afternoon? I saw you standing by my bed, and I immediately started to feel better." This was a confirmation that my visualizations and affirmations were working.

Creation requires several parts: visualization—composed of thought and feeling—the spoken word *(mantra)*—and you can also add gesture *(mudra)*. To be most effective, all three parts must be used together.

The I AM Presence is a ball of light, and the colors surrounding it are the wisdom and positive energy you have acquired from all your positive experiences throughout all of your lifetimes. This is not the physical aura you have around your head and physical body. Your I AM Presence is your spiritual aura. Its causal body is the sum total of all the Love, Wisdom, and Power you have acquired in all your lifetimes. It is a sun from the Great Central Sun, the Source of Creation, and the origin of our being.[12]

---

[12] The Great Central Sun is a location that is a focus of Consciousness at the heart of Creation.

Thus, one of the most powerful affirmations you can say is:

I Am a White-Fire Being from the heart of the Great Central Sun.

Chapter 5
The I AM Presence Returns

We are each like a drop from the cosmic ocean. If you take a hundred glasses of water from the Pacific Ocean, they all have the same essence as the ocean, but if you put that water in different colored glasses, the water will take on different colors. In a similar way, we all have the same light in our hearts, but it has taken on different colors as a result of our experiences and choices throughout all our lifetimes. This is why sometimes, when we meet another person, there is the feeling that we have met before, that this is someone from our family. There is a great closeness. The closer we get to the I AM Presence, to the God Self, the closer we feel to everyone. Ultimately, we are all the Family of God.

The middle emanation that comes from the I AM Presence we can call the Holy Christ Self, *Samboghakaya* (Sanskrit), or the soul—which is in contact with both the

I AM Presence and also the human self. It's an intermediary self and is the voice that speaks to us and relays the guidance of God. It is that Christ Self, between the human self and the God Self, that is near us all the time. When the lower self merges with the Christ Self, and then with the I AM Presence, that is the ascension. Thus, the human personality and soul eventually dissolve into the God Self, the I AM Presence, which is eternal.

There have been yogis in Tibet and China who accomplished this by dissolving the physical body into the Rainbow Body (Tibetan: *jalus)*, a process known in the West as Ascension. That requires a lifetime of work and dedication, and most of us in the West don't have the time or dedication for that. However, if we have cleared our karma we can still ascend from the etheric world once we are free of the physical body. The important thing is to learn the lessons we are here to learn and to become Masters on the Earth plane, with full access to our higher bodies— access to the I AM Presence—but to still live in these physical bodies in service to others. One of our Divine Lessons—learning Compassion—we can only learn in service to others.

It helps for us to realize that we are only here for a short time. It seems long, but in the realm of eternity—the span of all our lives—this life passes in the twinkling of an eye. When we awaken from this earth experience, it will be like having slept for a dream filled night. We can look at those dreams as ones we have chosen to experience. It was your will to come into the world of limitation and duality, a world where there is suffering, in order to gain compassion. What can keep us from getting pulled into that suffering, as victims, is the memory of who we truly are—the Presence of the Living God.

I had a second encounter with the I AM Presence. It was about 10 years after the first one. I was about to go through a time in my life that was going to be very trying—of course I didn't know that at the time—but one night I was awakened by a dazzling light above the house. I could see through the roof, which seemed to have disappeared—and there was an almost blindingly bright light in the sky falling toward the house. I thought that an airliner had exploded, and the debris was falling toward me. As it came closer, it got brighter and brighter, and I thought I was going to die. I was filled with fear and thought, "This is it—it's all over!"

I sat up to meet my death head on, but then the light disappeared. I sat there on my bed, breathless, wondering what happened. Then about 30 seconds later the light came back stronger than before, and I realized that it was my I AM Presence. The light was dazzling and terrifying, not harmonious and compassionate as the first time it appeared. I did not see the intermediary Christ Self, only the nearly blinding Light of my God Presence. As it came closer, my body became hotter—so hot that I broke into a sweat. I thought my body was going to combust and that I would ascend.[13] I have heard of cases of spontaneous combustion, where a body becomes incinerated in bed and in the morning only a few ashes remain. I thought that was going to happen, as the heat was almost unbearable. Soaked with sweat, I called out, "Why are you doing this to me?"

A voice came back:

I want you to know my power—that I am your God Presence and that I am with you always. I have the unlimited power to do anything. Never forget this.

The Presence disappeared and I collapsed back onto the bed.

Since then, whenever my human self has doubts and fears, I remember that experience with my I AM Presence. Saint Germain has

---

[13] There are over two hundred references over the past few hundred years of a phenomenon called spontaneous combustion, where most of the physical body is consumed by fire, but the surroundings are untouched by flame.

been calling my attention back to that experience. *Remember that Presence!* We need to work on becoming closer to the Presence at all times.

When we watch the news, it can be depressing, and we feel powerless. But, if you put your attention on your own God Presence, you will realize your unlimited power. Who you truly are is the Presence of God. You chose to have this human experience to learn things, but you are a powerful, Immortal Being. When these lessons are over, you will be free of this limitation. So, it is important to ask the Presence in meditation:

Why am I here now?
What am I meant to learn?

Then affirm:

I AM being shown what I need to work on in myself.

You will become aware of various human traits and tendencies, the *vrittis* and *kleshas,* magnetic imprints in the aura that have followed you through lifetimes and that have kept you imprisoned in the ego. These energies are like clouds in the aura that block the sun of the Presence. Invoke the Violet Consuming Flame, and then the Sword of Blue Flame of Archangel Michael to free yourself of these energies so that once again you may fully embody the radiant God being that you are.

Realize you are not here by accident. You chose to be here. You have a service here and that service can be put into action no matter where you are.

You can ask:

Beloved I AM Presence, show me how I can best serve the Will of God on Earth at this time.

Or:

I AM the Resurrection and the Life of my Divine Mission on Earth, now made fully manifest.

Chapter 6
Getting Rid of Karma

Your every thought is going out and affecting humanity. The more you meditate, the more powerful you become. We are Masters in training and this life is our training ground. I don't know any Ascended Master retreat where you can get the training you receive in daily life. The Masters can explain certain things to you in the retreats and transmit their energy to you, but the lessons in Mastery are learned right here on the Earth plane. One of the greatest lessons is just to be at peace—to observe yourself so you don't react to a situation. There is that old instruction: count to ten before you react to someone. You can observe ten breaths before you reply. During that time, you can think, "Do I really need to say what I'm thinking?" A lot of times you find that you don't. You can simply say, as my teacher Pearl often did, "Why bless you! Thank you for sharing your opinion." The great Tibetan Lama, Dilgo Khentsye, when confronted with a potentially irritating comment, disarmed the critic by saying simply, "Very interesting." Once an opponent feels heard, they usually drop the attack.

Some students have asked: *Do you have a technique to negate karma from past lives?"*

Karma can be good karma too you know. Karma just means action and the consequences of those actions. In fact, Karma is a common woman's name in Tibet, which is given in hopes that she will be active in doing good. It's our good karma to be meeting right now.

As far as negating bad karma, the best way to do that is through learning the lesson implicit in the action. We don't need to repay each karmic debt one by one. If you caused the suffering of a hundred people in a past life, you don't need to suffer for each of those hundred. If you have learned the lesson, you can move on. However, you might choose to have a future life in which you return to help one or more of those you injured.

Using the Violet Consuming Flame is an excellent way to dissolve negative karma. Remember, the essence of the Violet Flame is forgiveness. As Jesus said, *Forgive others if you want to be forgiven.*

If you're interested in another way to invoke the Violet Fire, I would suggest reading my two books on Violet Tara.[14] They present an advanced Tibetan *Vajrayana* (tantric) approach that not only transforms your own mind but also invokes the Violet Consuming Flame for the sake of humanity—dissolving and consuming mass karma. This is a tremendous service. I do this practice every morning when I awaken and at night before bed—also sometimes during the day. I affirm:

---

[14] *I AM the Violet Tara, Goddess of Forgiveness and Freedom* (Church of Seven Rays, 2019) and *I AM Violet Tara in Action, Lessons in Mastery* (Church of Seven Rays, 2020), both by Peter Mt. Shasta.

*I AM Violet Tara, blazing
the Violet Consuming Flame
throughout humanity, dissolving
and consuming all negative conditions
and restoring everyone to purity.
May all beings be forgiven.*

Chapter 7
Be God in Action

My mission and purpose is to testify to the truth of God within everyone—the reality of the being known as the I AM Presence. It is Who you are. Do not lose faith if you don't see it. There are many times I call for that Presence to come forth and would love to see that blazing ball of rainbow light above me. Even though I don't always see it when I desire, I know It is there. However, you have to learn to distinguish between the voice of the Presence and your own mind, which can only be learned through the self-discipline of meditation where you learn to quiet your mind.

When I go somewhere, or in whatever I do, I call for my Presence to be above and work through me. As I meditate, It comes closer and I feel Its energy coming down through my body. If you want to be protected, invoke that Divine Energy to come into you. That in itself is a form of

Qi Gong. Qi is energy. Gong means practice. So, it's an energy practice.

Every morning when I meditate...I awaken around four in the morning...I go up into the Christ Self and I am aware of the I AM Presence above me. The human self, Peter, disappears—and, as the Christ Self, I do inner work. I send that Light out where it's needed. Gradually, I start to become aware of Peter again, down in the physical body, and I start to come back down into the personal self. There's tremendous energy that comes down. It flows into my legs, my toes, into the tips of my fingers, and I become a radiant, energized being. That is the best thing to do for your health, well-being, and happiness. Sharing your Christ Self with others is the door to happiness.

A good way to start the day is to do the affirmations in my book, *I Am Affirmations and the Secret of their Effective Use*. It takes about twenty minutes to read through all the affirmations. If you do that first thing in the morning, or anytime during the day, you get rid of negative thought patterns and reprogram your mind positively. Feel what happens when you say these affirmations. Feel the energy come into you, then go out from your heart to bless humanity. Here are a few of those affirmations:

I AM the Great Divine Director of this day.

I AM the commanding, governing presence of God going before me throughout this day, bringing about the perfect Divine Plan in all activity.

I AM perfect health, vitality, eternal youth, beauty, and perfection forever, by the power of God which I AM.

I AM the Great Divine Director of all the governments of the earth, directing all governments to do the perfect thing and establish peace on earth right now.

I AM the Divine well-being of humanity.

I AM love and compassion filling the hearts of mankind.

I AM happiness come forth for all beings now, seeing that all receive what they need this very moment.

If you do the affirmations in that book it will change your day—and your life. You can also create some of your own affirmations. This is your destiny—to be a God in action. Just make sure these affirmations come from your God Self, not from ego desire for your life to manifest some fantasy. That's where meditation comes in, to help you surrender your personal desires to God, and for you to perceive God's desires for you. God will show you the Divine Plan for your life if you affirm in meditation:

O Great God Presence, Thy will be done in and through me now.

I AM being shown what to create.

Jesus gave two great commandments to his disciples at the last supper. He forewarned them, "I am going soon to my Father."

Not understanding, they answered, "Who is this Father you keep talking about? We've been hanging out with you for three years, but you still haven't introduced us to him. When do we get to meet him?"

Jesus answered, "You still don't get it, do you? Well, instead of trying to explain it once more, I'm going to give you these two commandments. Just try to practice these."

Love God with all your heart, all your soul, and all your mind.

Love your neighbor as you would love yourself.

That is really good advice for us on this path of Mastery.

Meditation

Close your eyes and commune with the I AM Presence. Sit up so your back is straight. Tuck your chin down slightly. Take a few deep breaths. Now breathe naturally, being aware of the inbreath and the outbreath, the rise and fall of your chest. Gradually feel the energy in the center of your chest. This is where the Sacred Flame from the I AM Presence, the *jyoti,* is anchored in your body. Your heart could not beat without this energy, nor could you take a breath. So, you are connected directly to God at every moment. Now say and feel:

God is breathing in me.

God is causing my heart to beat.

God lives in my physical body.

If I ask, *Who are you?* why do you point to the center of your chest when you say *Who me?* You don't point to your head or your shoulder. You instinctively point to the center of your chest. You point slightly to the right of the sternum (over the thymus gland). This is where the Sacred Flame is anchored.

There is a cord of light that goes from the Presence down through your Christ Self—through the top of your head and down through all your chakras. The Christ Self is a higher body, also called the Higher Mental Body, *Samboghakaya*, or soul. It is the intermediary between your human and God Self. It can go anywhere you put your attention. It is also your teacher, the *Vajra Guru* mentioned in Tibetan Buddhism.

Feel your Christ Self above you. Now send love to It and talk to It saying:

Beloved Christ Self, please teach me and help me dissolve my human imperfections. Transform them into Love, Wisdom, Mastery, and Compassion. Please teach me what I need to know. Reveal what I need to work on so that I may be of greater service to humanity. Every night, when I go to bed, teach me what I need to know. I ask to go forth and serve the Masters in their work for humanity.

Feel your oneness with your Christ Self. Affirm in the center of your being:

I AM a Living Christ.

"Christ" means anointed one. So, as that Higher Self enters us, we *are* anointed by Its Spirit. We are messengers of the most high living God. You become a Christ as you do this work for humanity. This work is your freedom as well as your protection. The more Love, Wisdom, Compassion, and Light you emanate, the more you are protected and the happier you become.

Imagine your Christ Self going higher, approaching this ball of rainbow-colored light that is your I AM Presence. And as you raise up into that Presence, your heart is filled with Love, and you say and feel:

I AM the Sun of God.

See and feel this radiant Sun in the center of your being, concentric circles of rainbow colors surrounding you. Immerse yourself in that Light and intensify it. You don't need to use will, just surrender and feel its radiance. It's as easy as getting into a hot tub, only you are now immersed in the Light of your I Am Presence.

Say and feel:

I AM a White Fire Being from the Heart of the Great Central Sun.

Immerse yourself in that visualization, meditating on your Light.

Gradually, you emerge from the I AM Presence and come back down into your Christ Self, which is above your physical body. That Self is in communication with you at all times. Listen to what it has to say. If you're not sure what it is trying to communicate, go with the feeling within you. Even though it is often called "going with the gut feeling," the feeling comes from the Flame anchored in the center of your chest. Call for the guidance to manifest within you by saying:

I AM being shown where to go and what to do—and I AM following that Plan.

As you start to go in a direction or take an action, ask inwardly, "Does this feel better or worse?" If it feels better, that's a sign you are going in the right direction or taking the right action. If the energy drops or feels worse, that is a sign to try an alternate action until the energy feels better. Pay attention to your energy and feelings, which give the impulse to right action. Feelings coming from the higher centers are not the same as emotions, which come more from the lower centers.

Come back down into awareness of your physical body. Feel that energy of God filling every cell. Feel the top of your head, likened to a thousand petalled lotus and known as the *sahasrara* chakra, now radiant with Light.

Then feel that Light come down into your third eye (*ajna* chakra) in the center of your forehead). Then bring the Light down into your throat center *(vishuddha* chakra), your power to create with speech. Lastly, bring the Light down into your heart center *(anahata* chakra), and feel love pouring forth to others.

Later, if you go for a walk, think, and feel:

*I AM the Presence of God walking.
God is walking in me.*

Feel God's energy in your thighs, knees, and feet. Feel there is a sun under each foot and say:

I AM blessing Mother Earth with each step.

You can also bring the energy to the *manipura* chakra in the solar plexus to give you physical vitality—or to any of the chakras, all of which are necessary for life and health if they function in harmony with each other under the direction of the God Presence. By doing Qi Gong practice you learn to circulate that life force throughout your body.

Close the meditation by bringing your attention back to your heart, sending love out to all.

My love goes out to everyone. As do the blessings of the Ascended Masters, who love you and are here with you. They are as close as your own heart. Every thought sent to Them is heard. Keep your attention on God in your heart. What your attention is upon, you become.

Chapter 8
What is the Name of God?
From a talk on November 9, 2020

What is the real name of God? How do you invoke that God into action? Some claim that the English statement "I AM" is God's name. However, as the modern English language is a relatively recent invention, that is impossible. Even Old English is unintelligible to us today. The I AM teachings existed prior to modern English, which did not fall out of the sky, but is a mixture of Proto-Indo-European, German, Scandinavian, French, Latin, Greek, and other languages, and has evolved over time.

The Vedic teachings of India pre-date the formation of English by at least ten thousand years. The ancient seers heard the *pranava*, which is the vibration of consciousness permeating creation. That sound is symbolized by the word *OM*, which gives only a hint of the real sound. God is invoked into action out of pure Consciousness through the use of affirmation. In Sanskrit that basic affirmation, I AM, is *Aham.* The full expression, I AM God, is *Aham Brahmasmi,* "I am Brahman."

The actual Hebrew name for God that appears in the Old Testament is the *Tetragrammaton,* the four-letter name: YHWH, which later became pronounced Yahweh, then Jehovah.[15] However, God was reported to have said in Exodus that his name was *Ayeh Asher Ayeh*, which in English is: *I will be what I will be.* Thus, God can be invoked by any name, in any language.

I AM is not a name but a statement of Being—as well as an invocation—a way to call that Being into action. What comes after those words is what you create or become. When you say I AM, you invoke

---

[15] It does not actually say in Exodus that God created Heaven and Earth, but that Elohim created Heaven and Earth—the Hebrew plural noun meaning Gods. Hence, it says: The Gods created Heaven and Earth.

your own God Presence into action. Say it in your native language to trigger God into action.

Because I was born in America, I say "I AM." From the time I was a child, I have become used to saying, "I am going to do this" or "I am going to create that." When I say I AM, it triggers God Consciousness, which is omniscient, omnipresent, and omnipotent, to come through me. But if I were born in France the natural thing would be to say "Je Suis." In Germany it would be "Ich Bin." It is the language you grew up with, or that is most natural to you, that best invokes God.

There is a discourse by Godfre Ray King given in 1932 in which it was written that Saint Germain said that I AM is God's name and should only be said in English. I find this highly unlikely as the English language is very recent, modern English only having come into being in the past 600 years. My teacher, Pearl, who was Godfrey's personal assistant, said that frequently he would make his own comments, toward the end of a discourse, after the Master had stopped dictating through him. However, the stenographer recording the discourse would often continue writing down what Godfre said, believing that they were still the words of the Master. Furthermore, a lady on the staff of the Saint Germain Foundation, Agnes "Sunny" Widell, said that on occasion Mrs. Ballard (Lotus Ray King) would change a discourse before it was published and insert comments that were her own opinion.

When Saint Germain apparently said, at the end of a discourse in 1932, not to use the expression *OM* or *Mani Padme Hum*, this was possibly Godfre's or Lotus's personal opinion rather than the words of the Master. Quite to the contrary, Saint Germain now guides many of his students to use Sanskrit mantras to teach concentration, meditation, and to activate the subtle spiritual centers.

One possibility that may explain this seeming discrepancy is the similarity of the 'sound of the English language expression I AM to its Sanskrit equivalent

Aham, pronounced: Ah Hum. They both mean I AM and sound somewhat similar.

In 1932, in the depths of the Great Depression, Pearl said that Saint Germain gave discourses whose main purpose was to release positive energy and uplift consciousness in America and bring the awareness of I AM into full use and acceptance. These statements of Oneness with God were given to raise the masses out of their depression and let them know that they are never separate from God. These were not intended to be the final and ultimate teachings to students of Light. Nothing was ever said in those discourses of the 1930s about attaining Enlightenment, which was certainly on the Masters' agenda, and already well known in the culture of India. However, the Masters knew that most of the students of Godfrey Ray King were not ready for those advanced teachings at that time.

Although Saint Germain did give a meditation to Godfre Ray King in *Unveiled Mysteries,* visualizing the Light, Godfre did not actively guide his students to practice this meditation. The only exception was a small group of students that included Pearl Dorris, to whom he gave private meditation instruction.

When Saint Germain gave these teachings in the 1930s, he wanted the students to reprogram their minds to be more positive and to work on improving society—rather than to become absorbed in the pursuit of personal Enlightenment.

Times have changed, and we can now pursue enlightenment while also realizing that others are a part of ourselves—and that we can simultaneously be involved in becoming enlightened while helping humanity. When in India in 1971, I saw the book *Meditation in Action* by the Tibetan lama, Trungpa Rinpoche, and I realized that this was the next step, becoming God Conscious while also being active in the world as a Master.

There are many people today practicing the *Advaita* Oneness teachings, which focus on returning to the consciousness of Oneness—from which we departed before entering the world of duality. That is a beautiful pursuit, but if you want to become a Master, just being in the Oneness will not achieve that. There are many yogis who became enlightened in past lives and who realized, after death, that they had only avoided duality, but not achieved Mastery over duality. Some of them have been reborn in this lifetime to be in relationship, to be parents, and to have jobs, so as to develop understanding of, and have compassion for, others. It's not the goal to say, "I'm in the Oneness and don't care what happens to others—that's their business." That's not why we're here. We were in God Consciousness before we were born. We came from the celestial realms and took birth in duality for a reason. That reason is to achieve Mastery, which is only attained through compassion. That compassion is realized when you truly see that all others, including their suffering, are a part of you.

Prior to the Saint Germain Foundation and the books that they published, there was little awareness of the I AM in the West. There are some affirmations in the

Gospels where Jesus uses the expression *I AM,* but no one used his affirmations for themselves—to call forth their own Divinity.[16] We can be grateful to Saint Germain and Godfre Ray King for bringing forth these teachings on how to invoke God in daily life for the benefit of humanity. These words, I AM, when said in your native language, are a key to unlock your Divine potential—for you call God forth into action. Feel the power—feel what happens when you say *I AM.*

What is God's real name and where did it originate? In the beginning, before creation, God was Consciousness beyond space and time. Out of this Consciousness came duality, space, and time. These concepts are well studied in India and

---

[16] My book, *I AM the Living Christ, Teachings of Jesus (*Church of the Seven Rays, 2017), gives a clearer interpretation of the Gospel of Matthew, showing how Jesus intended his affirmations to be used.

were written about extensively in the Vedas and the Upanishads thousands of years ago. As consciousness came forth out of the sleep of God, which lasted hundreds of millions of years, creation emerged. Creation dissolves, then comes forth again in great cycles. As Consciousness emerges from the silence, sound emerges. That primordial sound, the *pranava,* is symbolized by *OM.* The sound of the Indian instrument, the tambura, makes a sound somewhat similar to the primordial sound, but that sound cannot be duplicated in the physical realm. However, some yogis hear this sound in meditation.

Mantras are a means to call forth that Divine Perfection in oneself as well as the world. Out of the cosmic *OM,* the Sanskrit alphabet came forth. These are primordial sounds that every child makes regardless of their native language. Some of the vowel sounds are: *Ah, Ee, Ou, Eh, Ay, Oh, Ow,* and *Um;* while some of the consonant sounds are: *Kaka, Gaga, Ma, Papa, Baba,* and *Dada.* Children make these sounds spontaneously without being taught by their parents. Repetition of these primordial sounds used by Sanskrit facilitates Consciousness interacting with form.

Although I never taught my daughter to call me "Dada," I was stunned when, at around five months of age, she started saying that, then a month later, "Mama." Two fathers, one in South Korea and the other in Croatia, have both told me that their infants have begun calling them "Dada" without any prompting or English instruction. This spontaneous chanting of Sanskrit activates the subtle nervous system and develops coordination of spirit, soul, mind, body, and feeling, with speech.

Sanskrit awakens various aspects of consciousness, and when the sounds are linked together into mantras, they mean far more than their literal translated meaning. These statements are manifestations of Consciousness that affect, not only oneself, but the world. There are mantras to attain enlightenment, wisdom, and happiness, as well as to enhance mundane activities such as bathing, cooking, generating income, and for all aspects of life. Mantras are affirmations that invoke energy and Consciousness and have been practiced as a discipline in India for tens of thousands of years.

When you meditate on *I,* you are lifted into the Consciousness of your God Self. That is the vertical current of the Father Consciousness aligned with Divine Will. When you say AM, you invoke the Mother Consciousness to come forth from the heart—the Love principle that brings everything into creation. [17] There is nothing that exists on this Earth—that we can see and put a name on—that is not the

---

[17] The symbol of the cross was used to represent this interaction of the father and mother principles, which are united in the heart, long before the Catholic Church began to promote the crucifix with a shortened horizontal bar. Through the activity of the principles of father and mother, spirit and earth, we awaken to Wisdom and Mastery.

product of the Divine Mother and Divine Father in action. So, if we want to bring something into creation, or want to develop a quality within ourselves, we can say *I AM That*. Feel and meditate on that which you wish to manifest or become.

Say and feel:

I *AM the Light of the world*

Feel the energy come forth into activity to bless all creation.

I have been guided by Saint Germain to bring more of these teachings of the Far East, to the West, in a way that is simple and easy to understand. There should not be confusion over the name of God, whether it is I AM, Krishna, Yahweh, Allah, Wakan Tanka, or something else. There are thousands of names for God, but it is not the name but how to contact God, by whatever name, that is important. The amazing thing is that you are in contact with God at every moment, and only need to slow down the mind to be aware of that eternal and ever-present connection.

A thousand people could show up on the shore of the ocean with a thousand containers of different color. I might show up with a glass that is green. Someone else might show up with a glass that is blue or purple. There are thousands of shapes, colors, and sizes. Each person dips a container into the ocean and goes home and says, "I went to the ocean and brought some back and this is what it looks like. The ocean looks like this," and they show the ocean water, colored by their container, and they create a religion around the appearance of the ocean in their container. Then a neighbor also goes to the ocean with a different colored container and comes home and says, "No, you are wrong, I went to the ocean, and it looks like this." They are all talking about the same ocean. Let's not get caught up in the illusions created by the containers, and instead appreciate the Truth that all have in common. Each person can pray and ask within:

What should I call God?

By what method should I contact God?

What is God trying to teach me?

Chapter 9
What Is the Self?
From a talk on February 24, 2021

There are many paths up the mountain. Many of these paths deal with the problem of trying to experience Oneness while also becoming a Master in duality.

A student asked me: *How can we be in the Oneness but at the same time also be in the world in relationship with others?*

The path you should follow is the one that starts where you are standing—the path in front of your feet. During your life many different paths may appear. Of course, if you were born in Tibet you'd be studying Tibetan Buddhism. You wouldn't have had exposure to anything else. Here in the West, we now have exposure to many paths, and everyone is saying their path is the best. All traditional paths have their place and offer something. The important thing is to be true to the path you're on and not mix paths together—then you get a soup that's very watery and doesn't nourish you. If you're doing Zen meditation and start passionately singing the names of Hindu Gods, a devotional path known in Sanskrit as *bhakti*, that's a mixture that's not going to yield good results. Do one or the other. In my own life I have practiced both, but not at the same time.

If you go totally into the Oneness like Ramakrishna often did, you're just not aware of yourself, let alone of anyone else—you can't drive a car, go to work, or be in relationship, because there is no "other" to be in relationship with. There is simply a blissful emptiness. I have experienced that and there was no awareness of self or anything. It's timeless awareness, but you can't live in that and be outwardly functional. That is where mindfulness practice is needed. We can be anchored in the Oneness, but still live in relative awareness of our surroundings and the roles in which we want to participate in life.

If you're going to function in the world you need to be aware of self and other, not to mention the need to look both ways before crossing the street. Even though I know the Consciousness in you is related to the Consciousness in me, drops from the same ocean, still you are one drop and I am another. If I am driving a car in the US, I have to stay on the right side of the road. That is admitting that there is such a thing as duality. I need to be mindful while driving. What side of the street am I on? Are there any other cars coming my way? How fast am I going? Yet, I can still be aware of my thoughts and emotions while realizing that God is the one driving—and that it is God's car. That is being mindful. You can be in the world but not of the world. No matter what your spiritual path, relationship entails being mindful—aware of self, other, and the Absolute—all simultaneously. That takes real Mastery.

Another question I was recently asked is: *Does the I AM Consciousness resemble what the Tibetan Buddhists call* rigpa (primordial awareness)?

As Lao Tzu said, *the truth that can be written is not the full truth.* We can only talk about the nature of ultimate awareness using words that are limited. Some people study the I AM but it's all in their heads. Buddhists say you have to kill the sense of "I" to attain awareness of your true nature. What they mean is to kill identification with the ego—the "me," the attachment to the little self that clings to delusion. Dzogchen says you have to get beyond all sense of a separate "I" to realize the fundamental ground of all awareness known as *rigpa*. The sense of "I" flows out of that awareness—the realization of an individual self who is aware. Then comes the desire of that self to express, which happens through thought, feeling, and the expression, I AM. So, I AM flows out of *rigpa*.

In the book, *Chop Wood, Carry Water* it says that before you are enlightened you have to chop wood and carry water, and after you're enlightened you still have to chop wood and carry water.[18] But you do it with a different consciousness. You are aware of the field of unlimited consciousness, yet mindful of your role in relative reality at the same time. That is Mastery.

A few years ago (2015) I was on a three-year retreat in a cabin in the mountains of upstate New York. Two cords of firewood were delivered in a big pile, and I had to carry the logs inside and stack them in the woodshed so that when the snow fell I would have firewood to heat my cabin. I knew it was going to take two or three days to move all the firewood inside. I didn't really want to do this, but I said to myself, "I can make this a meditation. Instead of complaining, I will observe each armful of firewood in the same way as I would observe my breath in

---

[18] *Chop Wood, Carry Water: A Guide to Finding Spiritual Fulfillment in Everyday Life,* by Rick Fields (Jeremy P. Tarcher, Inc., 1984)

shamatha meditation, or the way I would observe each syllable if reciting a mantra."

I thought, "The wood is God. It was given to me by God. I am the Presence of God carrying the wood. Burning the wood will be a celebration of God, and it's going to keep God alive during the cold winter that is coming."

With each armload of firewood, I observed myself. I had the choice: to be impatient, angry, and frustrated, or I could be in a state of equanimity—even Enlightenment. So, I got myself into that frame of mind and I saw this work as a meditation. It lasted three days and I had a high experience.

Is the mind really like a mirror as the Buddhists claim? That is another question I was recently asked. After a while you perceive that everything is a reflection of yourself. If you become angry at another person but can at the same time still your human mind to some degree, you see that the other person is mirroring your own anger, and you can give gratitude to that mirror for showing what you need to work on.

Gradually you begin to move into the higher consciousness that allows you to see the Cosmic Mirror. In Tibetan Buddhism they talk about the three *Kaya's*, or bodies. The physical body is known as the *Nirmanakaya*; the Higher Mental Body is known as the *Sambhogakaya*; and the I AM Presence is the *Dharmakaya*. This highest body is sometimes portrayed in Tibetan art as Amitabha Buddha, the God of Infinite Light.

Some lamas who haven't actually experienced these higher bodies think the *Dharmakaya* is just a level of consciousness. Even though *kaya* means body, they don't realize that, even though made of Light, the *Dharmakaya* is an actual body that is your True Self. You also have another body which we sometimes call the soul or higher mental body. That's the Sambhogakaya. So, these bodies are real, not just states of consciousness. You do have a permanent self which is the Dharmakaya, although most Buddhists won't admit to anything as being permanent. What is impermanent is our human personality with all of its attachments. Even the Dharmakaya turns its focus inward, seeming to disappear, during what the Vedas call the Night of God. According to the *Vishnu Purana*, God is awake for a kalpa, which is 4.32 billion earth years, then sleeps for another kalpa, and so on.[19] When God goes to sleep, the sense of self disappears. All

---

[19] A Kalpa has a subdivision known as a Yuga. We are currently in the Kali Yuga, which will reportedly last 430,000 years. The Vedas claim this age began with the death of the Avatar known as Krishna, about 5,000 years ago, so still has a long way to go. Human civilization has risen, developed technologically, and dissolved many times, sometimes ending in nuclear war. The Indian epic Mahabharata contains many references to spaceships known as vimana, which fired missiles such as the Brahmastra, causing great devastation and making the land uninhabitable for many generations.

awareness of ego is gone. That's what the Buddhists mean by saying the self is not permanent, but eventually that God Self, of which we are part, will awaken again and come forth into incarnation to realize other goals. It is the human ego and its attachments that are truly impermanent.

Many people ask Buddhist teachers why they say that the self is not permanent when they talk so much about reincarnation. Many of them search for *tulkus*, reincarnated lamas. If there is no permanent self, then what is being reincarnated?

I have asked several Lamas, "You say there's no permanent self, so why are you praying to Buddha and Padmasambhava, who were real people like us? They are still around if you're praying to them, right?"

They didn't like that question. They didn't want to discuss it because there is no answer that fits the official dogma.

There are different levels of realization leading to God Consciousness. You can be aware of yourself as a God Being, and then move on into Cosmic Consciousness, where there appears to be no self—all individuality having merged into the Oneness.

The funny thing is this happened to me in a barn in upstate New York while shoveling horse manure. I was using the pitchfork for about an hour when I went spontaneously into a state of Cosmic Consciousness.

I don't know how long I was in that bliss of pure absorption known as *samadhi*. Gradually, I started to come back. The sense of self started to come back—the awareness of being somebody. As the sense of *I* fully returned, I saw that I was standing in a barn with a pitchfork raised in the air, the horse looking at me with a questioning look in its eyes.

There are different levels of *samadhi* (absorption in pure consciousness). But this was the highest, there being no self— I had merged into the Light of pure Being, Consciousness, and Bliss *(satchitananda)*, accompanied by the sound *OM*. This was not the *OM* that is spoken or chanted but more like the sound of the Indian instrument, the Tambura.

Just doing something rhythmic like watching your breath, looking at the river, like Siddhartha (in the novel by that name by Hermann Hesse), or even watching a spot on the wall—anything that slows your mind down—can enable you to experience profound states of higher consciousness.[20] But you can't function in the world in the highest state because there is no awareness of the world.

The key is to learn how to be in relative reality in the world while also being aware of the sea of Oneness in which you exist, especially when you have to work with

---

[20] Ram Dass said that he saw a very enlightened woman at one of his talks, and when he asked her what her spiritual practice was, she said, "crocheting." This would be called meditation with support, using an object or method to still the mind and achieve meditative absorption. The highest level of samadhi, such as what I experienced, is meditation without support. You are simply there.

other people—maybe people you don't like or who don't like you. You know that, despite appearances, they are part of yourself. This is what we need to work on. It's not just thinking, "I'm going to get enlightened and get out of here so I don't have to deal with these people."

Realize that to be a Master, a *bodhisattva,* you must stay engaged with humanity and know that all beings are part of yourself.[21]

In the *Metta* practice, to generate loving kindness you become aware of the suffering of others, then transform that within yourself by sending out Light to those who need liberation. I think there needs to be more emphasis on generating love and compassion, not just thinking, "I'm going into Oneness and goodbye."

With all this political intrigue that the news media are reporting, if you take the

---

[21] *Bodhisattva,* one who has vowed to attain enlightenment for the sake of other beings and, although enlightened, to remain in samsara (delusion) until all others are also liberated.

position of one side against the other, then you are denying that the other side is also a part of you. Most politics is ignorance, used to set people against each other so they can be controlled. We have to forgive people their ignorance. We also have to feel compassion for them because they are creating future suffering for themselves when the consequences of their actions return—which they will. Know that those who suffer today are experiencing that mostly as a consequence of their past actions.

The first step in meditation is to still the mind. I've done nine-day *Vajrayana* (tantric Buddhist) retreats where you generate the presence of the Deity continuously for 9 days. Ideally, the first step is to go into a state of timeless awareness. That can take years to learn, but the lamas assume you know this already. Then, you imagine the Deity in front of you until it appears real. This is the generation phase. You generate all this love and devotion for the Deity until it manifests for you as a real being. Then in the completion phase, it merges with you and you become the Deity. You say and feel, "I AM the Deity."

This is very interesting because I studied the I AM teachings for many years, and then when I went to study Tibetan Buddhism the lamas said that to say "I AM" is an ego trip and not to do it. The Americans were all chanting in Tibetan, not understanding what they were chanting. During a break, I asked, "What are we doing?" The guy sitting near me said, "I don't know, but it must be good for us." I said, "Look, don't pay any attention to me, but I'm going to read the English." When the practice began again, I came to the line, "I am Vajrasattva." In other words, we were chanting, "I am the Deity."

I was shocked to see the I AM teachings right in the middle of a Vajrayana Buddhist practice! In this completion phase you are the Deity sending Love, Compassion, Light, and Healing out to the world.

The last stage is to then dissolve the visualization, so people don't go around thinking forever that they actually *are* the Deity.[22] The New Age is full of ego-centered people who feel they are special—which is no doubt why the Tibetan lamas stress so much to Westerners to dissolve the sense of "I." What they really mean is to dissolve the attachment to the ego, the delusion that it is real.

---

[22] During my time living in and around the town of Mount Shasta, at least four women have told me in private that they are Mary Magdalene reincarnated. They can't all be her, but all can feel oneness with her. In Tibetan Buddhism there is the concept of an emanation of a Deity. One can be so aligned and in tune with a particular Being that one feels no separation and can act as an emissary. I explain how one can attain this in my book, *I AM the Violet Tara, Goddess of Forgiveness and Freedom* (Church of the Seven Rays, 2019).

Chapter 10
Advice for Difficult Times
From a talk on April 8, 2021

A lot of people are asking,

Why am I here and for what purpose?

The Masters have heard your calls. They are aware of each and every one of you. After I returned from India and was offered ascension, Saint Germain raised me above the Earth so I could look down on the suffering. It was almost unbearable. I had no choice but to remain on Earth.

My heart goes out to you. The Masters are aware of you. Please, please do not think of leaving before your time. This is the time for which you were born. Your every thought affects the rest of humanity. Humanity needs you!

We are all in the great "inner-net" of life. Just like the internet, we are all connected inwardly through our hearts and minds. You are all affecting each other, so please turn your attention to the

Light—the Light within. Put your attention on the God Presence, which is within and above you. Whether you visualize that Light as what Jesus called the Father, or the Divine Mother, or the Higher Self, the I AM Presence—however you want to think of God and by whatever name—God hears you. You could not take a breath without God, for it is the God Power in your body that causes your lungs to expand and contract. It is the God Power that beats your heart. Your life is given to you by God and is a part of God. Please do not relinquish that gift until it has been appreciated to the fullest. Sometimes that involves pain and suffering, but that is how we grow. Please know that you are not alone. If you are in need, reach out to your friends and share your feelings, talk to people you have not spoken to in a long time, for they are suffering too—and they need you. By connecting, we help each other.

These are unusual times—even apocalyptic. There is tremendous Light coming into the Earth. Some people perceive that as a threat and want to retreat into the darkness of governmental control and oppression. We have the choice to go into a higher world. This is the New Heaven and the New Earth spoken of by the ancient prophet Isaiah, who said, I *saw a new Heaven and a new Earth, for the first Heaven and the first Earth had passed away.*

To enter that New Heaven and New Earth, we must purify ourselves—get rid of negative thoughts and emotions and turn to the Light. As we gain compassion for one another—the Great Ones, the Ascended Masters, and great Cosmic Beings, can raise us into that Kingdom of Heaven which is opening to us. Then we will be together in that Kingdom of Light, perhaps even sooner than we think.

The Masters know what is happening on the Earth, as do our Space Brothers and Sisters who are our ancestors. Saint Germain told me of the times to come. He said that a great event would occur and that those who had purified themselves sufficiently would be taken by great spaceships to a higher frequency world within the Earth that is a place of great beauty, harmony, and light. This is the New Heaven and New Earth, which some call Shamballa.

In 1975 Saint Germain took me there for a brief visit. This Inner Earth was as beautiful as the outer Earth, with rivers, forests, flowers, and an inner sun. He told me that the times were coming for which the Masters and our Space Elders have prepared. They regard us, who are on the Earth at this transitional time, as great warriors of Light, but they need each of us to call forth more Light, Love, and Compassion—which allows them to intercede on our behalf.

Please do not dwell on the stories in the news, but rather dwell on the Kingdom of Heaven into which you are ascending as you turn your attention inward. Still your mind in meditation and get in touch with that Kingdom of Light and Love within yourself, the doorway to which is in the center of your chest. To do this, start by simply observing your breathing. I know it sounds simple, but for tens of thousands of years the great yogis of India and Tibet have used this practice to achieve inner peace, enlightenment, and liberation.

Meditation practice:

As you breathe, feel the rise and fall of your chest. It is best to keep your eyes partially open. Do not control your breathing. Simply feel the inbreath and the outbreath—the rise and fall. When your mind wanders to something like a noise, pain in your body, or a thought, just label that "thinking," and come back to observe your breathing. Gradually the flow of thoughts will slow, and you will feel inner peace and equanimity. Then observe yourself and ask:

Who is conscious of this process?

Your mind may not stop completely at first, but as it slows down you become aware—aware of a vast consciousness observing your mind, observing your process. It is observing your ego and its fears, doubts, and suffering. It is that Observer with which you begin to identify. At that point, free of attachment to the self, you begin to enter the New Heaven and the New Earth.

As you sit with your mind still, you observe everything from a broader perspective. You see that you are not your physical body, not your emotions, not your thoughts. You are Universal Awareness looking down on your human self and on the entire human condition. This awareness of your Eternal Self does not die, but transitions from lifetime to lifetime. Finally, after all lessons have been learned, it is absorbed back into the Oneness Consciousness of the God Self— what the Tibetans call the *Dharmakaya,* the Sanskrit word meaning Truth Body. In meditation you can affirm:

I am now one with that Source, one with the Presence of the Living God I AM.

Know that this same consciousness is in everyone, regardless of their state of realization. This is not something you say from the ego. It's an awareness that takes you beyond the limited self. In that awareness you will realize Who, or rather *What,* you are. Then call to your God Self to know your mission on Earth.

This is a time of great transition. Please put your faith in the Great Presence that you *really are.* Know that many others are going through the same thing as you. Let us unite together as a family and help each other. Even if you don't know anyone, even if you're living alone or in the street, you are connected with humanity. You are connected with Jesus, Saint Germain, Mother Mary, the Ascended Masters, Angels, Cosmic beings, and always with your own I AM Presence. Our hearts are all connected. By accepting that connection with God, you open the door for God to come to you and work through you. At any point you can say:

Dear God, please help me!

Use whatever name for God that resonates with you and Your God, the I AM Presence will hear you calling as surely as if you rang the doorbell to the gates of Heaven. God will respond in whatever way is needed. That might not be as a flash of light or some other way you wish at the moment, but in perfect Divine Order you will receive the help you need. That response might come as a feeling, inner prompting, dream, phone call, a bird passing overhead, or simply an intuition.

As it says in Mathew 7:7:

Ask and it will be given to you; seek and you shall find; knock and the door will be opened unto you.

Be still and know that I AM is the Presence of the Living God. Whatever you say with the consciousness of I AM, you will bring forth into the world.
Say and feel as you go forth:

I AM Love

Think of someone in need of healing and say and feel:

I AM Healing going forth to that person.

If you need guidance say and feel:

I AM being guided and directed now and at all times. I AM the Great Divine Director of my life and world.

To bring peace to the world say and feel:

I AM the Peace which passeth all human understanding now come forth and fully established on the Earth.

For grounding, say and feel:

> *I AM God on Earth in this body right here now.*

In the stillness, feel the Peace, and know that your affirmations are bearing fruit.

Not only does my Love go with you, but also the Love of the Great Ones who enfold you this very moment. Blessings, many Blessings always.

Chapter 11
Meditation in Action at a Cafe
From a talk on April 16, 2012

I call this my Latte Meditation. I get up in the early morning before Sunrise to meditate. Then I walk up Mount Shasta Boulevard to Seven Suns Cafe to meet my friends and possibly do inner work. If I am sitting alone I use simple affirmations in the meditative state to benefit other people as well as the community. This is meditation in action, a form of what the Tibetan Buddhists call *skillful means*.

I did Vipassana meditation earlier in the morning. Once I am in that expanded consciousness, I come here and apply skillful means to bring that expanded awareness into daily life, and to bring benefit to others. I work silently so as not to attract attention. Nobody knows what I'm doing. I keep observing my breath to keep my mind still and my attention inward on my Buddha Nature. Depending on the inspiration of the moment, I say and feel:

*I AM the Living Light radiating out
to this cafe, blessing all who enter.*

*I AM the commanding, governing
Presence going forth to bring about
perfect Peace, Love, Wisdom, Harmony,
and the Ascended Master Divine Plan.*

*I AM the Presence of God blessing
that person....*

*I AM the Invincible Guard fully
established, sustained, and maintained,
about this cafe.*

*I AM the Presence of God in harmony
with the Ascended Masters, bringing into
this cafe the people I can benefit.*

*I AM being shown how to help those who
are sent to me.
I AM doing what is needed here.*

*I AM blessing all wherever I go,
in whatever way I can.*

*I AM Divine Healing going forth
to heal all.*

*I AM the Resurrection and the Life
of everyone here.*

It's quite simple, yet very powerful. You can do this kind of work wherever you are as long as you first establish the inner focus. Then say the words within yourself and release their power. In the space between affirmations, return to silent awareness. This is meditation in action—a form of Mastery.

Chapter 12
Meditation on Consciousness
From a talk on November 22, 2020

I'd like to say that we're all in this together because we are all parts of the One, from the same Source. We are all connected inwardly, drops from the same Ocean of God Consciousness. There appear to be Atlantic, Pacific, and Indian Oceans, yet these separate oceans are connected. If you take drops out of these oceans, the drops are still connected with their Source and with each other. So are we all connected.

In *Leaves of Grass*, the famous book of poems by Walt Whitman (1819-1892), he made the analogy of people to blades of grass. Each of us is a separate leaf while also a part of the whole lawn. We are individual condensations from the Great Source, which is beyond name and form, beyond time and space:

*In all people I see myself,
None more and none...less.
I exist as I AM, that is enough....*

-Walt Whitman, *Song of Myself*

When I was a little boy, my mother was very proud of her diamond engagement ring. It glittered with rainbows. But I was not impressed, so one morning I said, "Mom, look outside at the lawn. There is a drop of dew on every blade of grass, and a rainbow glittering in each drop. Each of those rainbows is as beautiful as the one in your diamond ring." In fact, I thought the rainbow in the dew was more beautiful as it appeared magically every morning and was free. It was a miracle.

An even greater miracle is in each of us. Like the dew, we are condensations of God Consciousness. We are each capable of inspiring in others that awe at the Presence of God. Like the moisture in the air that condensed in the morning as dew, ages ago God Consciousness condensed as our I AM Presence.

That Presence sends a tube of light down into the etheric body, which some call the Christ Self or Soul (Sanskrit: *Jiva)*. This soul is with you all the time, waking or sleeping, and you can call It into action. The tube of light descends further down through the top of your head and is anchored in the center of your chest, close to the sternum where it feeds a flame, called the *Jyoti* in Sanskrit. This flame, which is a focus of Love, Wisdom, and Power, keeps you alive. It can also be sent forth to awaken, bless, and heal others.[23]

---

[23] I was blessed with a transmission of God Consciousness in such a manner by the Indian saint Anandamayi Ma (1896-1982) when I met her on the street near the Jagannath Temple in Puri, India. Her Sanskrit name translates as "Bliss Permeated Mother." She was a friend of Paramahansa Yogananda, whom he wrote about in his *Autobiography of a Yogi*. The complete story of my four life-changing meetings with her are in the first part of my autobiography: *Adventures of a Western Mystic: Search for the Guru, Book I* (Church of the Seven Rays, 2013)

As you feel love, that love goes out to everyone. That's why the greatest service you can do right now is to love yourself. I don't mean to love your illusory ego self, but your God Self. That affects everyone. Right now, what you are experiencing is going out to the people who live nearby as well as to those who live in your city and country—even the whole planet. We are changing Earth at this moment—transmuting negative into positive, hate into Love, material into spiritual consciousness.

We all agreed to be here at this point in time and space to experience this God Dominion. Instead of dwelling on the negative, we can put our attention on the positive. Putting our attention on God is the greatest service we can render. This affects the whole planet. As you do the next meditation you will become like a wi-fi router, transmitting God Consciousness everywhere.

I call on the Ascended Masters to be with us. Actually, they are calling on us to render this service to humanity—inspiring us to come together to do this for them. It is a service for us as well, for what you send out comes back to you amplified many times. If you want Love, give Love. If you want Compassion, feel Compassion for others. No person, no guru, no church, no teaching, has the whole absolute Truth. As the Chinese poet Lao Tzu said in the *Tao Te Ching* in the 4th century BCE:

> *The truth that can be written*
> *is not the truth.*

A teacher can only point the way.

Let us now go inward and experience the reality of God within. Go beyond duality, beyond time and space, into Pure Consciousness.

Meditation:

Close your eyes and feel the inbreath and outbreath, the rise and fall of your chest. This will help slow down your mind. Just breathe naturally and feel the rise and fall—very simple. The breath works like a silent mantra that is going all the time. As your mind slows, you realize there is a space between thoughts. It is the wandering thoughts that keep you linked to your body and ego like a puppy on a leash that wants to go this way and that. Make your mind obey and rest in the stillness. Then realize within yourself:

> *I AM not my body—*
> *I AM not my mind—*
> *I AM not my emotions.*
> *I AM the Observer*
> *watching these.*

Identify with that Observer. Imagine that you are in a room created by your Consciousness. Your mind is a ball of Conscious Light in the center of that room, expanding outward...expanding beyond the room. The Light of your Mind expands beyond the town, the city, the country, beyond all boundaries...even beyond the Earth...radiating into space. That ball of Consciousness is becoming One with

All...and you realize that you are Everything. Sit with that for a while.

As you emerge from that expanded Consciousness, become aware again of yourself as an individual, a Ray from the Great Central Sun, an individual Ray of God. Now you can express yourself as a Creator by using the words, *I AM.* That statement calls forth the Source. When you say or think *I AM* in your native language, you call forth Consciousness to manifest in whatever form you invoke by the words you say after *I AM.* What you say, feel, and visualize is what you bring into being.

It is important to say *I AM* from the Center of your God Consciousness, not from the ego. Some people use the I AM to create from ego and end up with conditions that don't serve them, or with unnecessary possessions that weigh them down. As we are aligned with Divine Will, we can use I AM to bring Peace and Love on Earth. To do that we can say from the heart:

I AM Peace on Earth.

I AM Peace radiating out into the world.

I AM the Presence of God radiating Peace to my brothers and sisters and all God's children.

I AM the Peace which passeth all human understanding.

I feel gratitude to be here at this time. Out of the great sea of Eternity, I have come forth at this moment in space and time to be present among humanity on planet Earth to experience what I am experiencing now, and to grow in Mastery from the experience.

It is like a movie in which we volunteered to be characters. We are all heroes and heroines in this great movie directed by God. Play your part well, yet remember it is a movie in which you chose to participate and from which you can learn. From observing the movie of your life, you can learn how to help others. We chose to take on this particular role in which God, out of infinite Grace, has allowed us to play—to take on the illusion of not being God so that we can have the joy of remembering once again that we are God. Play your part masterfully. Know that this is a movie that will someday end, after which you will return to the Source.

Say, know, and feel:

I AM the presence of God at this point in space and time, fully conscious of the role I AM playing in this Divine Illusion, and I AM playing my part well.

The Ascended Masters, who were all once human like us, are our elder brothers and sisters. Jesus, Saint Germain, Mother Mary, Quan Yin, and the Taras, are all aspects of ourselves in this great schoolroom of life. I feel the heart in each and every one of you. I feel your love and your gratitude because I am a part of you, and you are a part of me in the great sea of

God Consciousness—the Father/Mother God in which we are One.

Remember, a call to any Ascended Master is a call to all of them. The Ascended Master who can best help you is the one that will respond. They might not come visibly, or in person, or speak to you audibly, but they are with you—especially your own I AM Presence. You are connected at every moment with your God Self. That I AM Presence hears your every word, every thought, and every feeling. Turn to that Source for what you need and claim what is yours. Albert Einstein said:

Reality is merely an illusion, albeit a very persistent one.

Within the illusion we learn to be performers and artists. Every artist paints a slightly different picture, even of the same flower. We chose to manifest as individual beings for the greater joy of God—because God did not want just one type of flower, but a multitude: roses, lilies, orchids, and sunflowers. God manifested as the many for a reason. Each of us is a particular, unique flower, which should be appreciated.

When you go to bed at night, you can leave your body and go into higher worlds, to planes of being on higher frequencies where there are Enlightened Beings waiting to help you. You can go to the Ascended Masters and receive training to learn how to help others. Even now, on other levels, and at different frequencies, you are helping people at various places on the Earth. We are living in multiple frequencies and bodies simultaneously. In meditation, and when you go to sleep at night, you can consciously go forth and help people from those levels.

To facilitate this, before you go to sleep, meditate, and then ask to merge with your Christ Self to go forth in service to those in need. Ask to be invincibly protected by Archangel Michael's Sword of Blue Flame and his Legions of Light. The way you learn is by doing. Call God into action in whatever form is most natural and that suits you best.

Know that we are all connected on the inner planes and that the Ascended Masters are with you. They are not only aware of you, They love you and are there for you. *I love you too, and bless you.*

Chapter 13
The Pearl of Great Price

The meditation that Pearl taught me is so special that it should be taught in school. It's very simple yet incredibly powerful. I had to travel all over the world, seeking teachers, and exploring many paths, before I was ready to learn this meditation.

I went to Tibet and India, spending months with the guru of Ram Dass, Neem Karoli Baba. I also spent time with Anandamayi Ma, the "Bliss Permeated Mother," and also with the avatar Sathya Sai Baba, as well as with many *siddhas* (realized beings) in the Himalayas. I endured great hardship and spared no expense to find enlightened beings, and although I saw many miracles, none taught me what a little old lady taught me in a small logging town in northern California.

Pearl did not live in an ashram or temple but in a normal neighborhood in a small house at the end of a road. This was before the Internet and there had been no ads or articles about her. People found out about her by word of mouth. She looked a bit like Yoda, in the film *Star Wars*, but was a 65-year-old housewife, and the teacher that Saint Germain sent me to meet.

The story of how Saint Germain appeared before me in Muir Woods, in physical form, is told in my autobiography *Apprentice to the Masters* and also in several of my YouTube videos. At that time Saint Germain told me: *The first person you meet in Mount Shasta will tell you what to do next.*

After I arrived in the town of Mount Shasta, I was having breakfast at The Breakfast House on the main street, and a young man who owned the health food store came up to me and said, "You're supposed to see a lady by the name of Pearl."

The young man said, "You can use my phone."

I went to his health food store around the corner and phoned Pearl.

"Come right up," she said.

When I got to her house, I knocked on the door. The door was opened by a sweet little lady who looked like she was somebody's grandmother.

"I've been expecting you," she said.

"How could you be expecting me?" I asked, puzzled, as I had never heard of her.

"The Master Saint Germain came to me this morning and said he was sending someone to see me."

"That's interesting," I said in shock.

"What brought you here?" she asked, giving me a penetrating look.

I told her how Saint Germain had materialized in front of me in Muir Woods. I had been thinking of leaving my body the way yogis can do in India. I had been living in the Himalayas with a yogi who was getting ready to do just that. I didn't care about living in the world anymore. In New York, I had lived the fast life that was supposed to bring happiness, but it hadn't—so I was ready to go to the higher worlds, some of which I had already experienced. Saint Germain had offered me the choice to leave the physical plane, but after he showed me the suffering of humanity on Earth, I had said that I would stay to help out. Then he said that he wanted my assistance, but that first I would need training. For that training, he sent me to Pearl, former assistant to Godfre Ray King, founder of the I AM Activity. Pearl taught me how to do consciously what Anandamayi Ma had transmitted to me on a street in Jagannath Puri in India.

Pearl explained that there is a place in the center of your chest, under the sternum, known in Sanskrit as the *Jyoti*. You can tap on it and say, "Wake up, God." Of course, God is always awake, but it's your mind that needs to wake up. Your mind needs to wake up to its being an aspect of God. As you merge with that awake Self, you begin to ascend, to attain the Rainbow Body.[24] Pearl stressed that this Ascension can also be attained after the change called "death," so there is no need to go into a cave or do drastic austerities to ascend the physical body in the manner of Tibetan and Chinese yogis.

Pearl's Open-Eyed Meditation

This is a practice that accelerates Ascension. The method is incredibly simple and is available at all times—but it needs to be practiced with someone else who is also a dedicated practitioner. It is a

---

[24] I have a photograph of the Sixteenth Karmapa performing a meditation ritual in which you can see right through the upper half of his body. One of my teachers, known as Master Yu Tian Jian (1951-2011), told me that he was present in the mountains of China when his teacher, Hui Ling, ascended. He witnessed flashes of light of all the colors of the rainbow. When he went back to where his teacher had been standing, only his hair and fingernails were left—the body was gone.

form of Buddhist tantra in which you realize the unbroken awareness between yourself and the other person—seeing both as Deities who are aspects of the One.

Both participants keep their eyes open, not staring, but seeing each other. Let your eyes go out of focus and bring your attention to the center of your chest—to what, in India, they call the *Jyoti,* the Sacred Flame—God's Temple in your physical body. Keep the focus right there on that sacred altar.

Feel the breath going in and out, the rise and fall of your chest. That process slows down the mind. As the mind slows, one enters the doorway into the Sacred Temple of Consciousness where that Sacred Flame resides. See the Light of the Flame glow brighter as it becomes a sun. As we sit across from each other there are now two suns shining light to each other.

If you have a hard time visualizing a sun, think of Love. Think of someone you love and feel that love radiating out from the center of your being. The more you think about it, the stronger it becomes. The

Love and Light are two aspects of Divine Consciousness. Say and feel:

I AM the living Light.

Meditate on *I* and that will take you to your center. Then meditate on:

What am I?

That will take you to your God Self – from which you can call God into action with the words *I AM.*

Your body is not really physical. Although it appears physical, scientists will tell you that your body is 99.9 percent empty space. The remaining one tenth percent is energy vibrating at a certain frequency. There's no such thing as a solid. Everything is form, energy, and vibration. You are really not a solid being, but Consciousness.

When you do this meditation with another person, keep your eyes open, without staring, and you will start to see light around their head, and then around their whole torso. Allow your eyes to go out of focus.

When I say *I AM the Living Light,* I send a beam of light from my heart to your heart, and you can do the same. We become two suns sending light to each other. We see each other as embodiments of God. It's very beautiful, God beholding God.

Say and feel:

I AM the Presence of God blessing you.

I AM Divine Love pouring forth to you.
I AM the Living Christ in Action here.

A ray of Light passes between our hearts. This is what is meant in India by the greeting, *Namaste:* The God in me greets the God in you.

You can also say:

I AM the Healing Presence of God,
healing you.

As the practice continues and you hold your attention on your Source, the Light perceived within and around the other person, and even in the surrounding environment, may visibly increase. This luminosity can increase to the point where the other person seems to dissolve in Light. The practice may be ended by clasping your hands together, palm to palm, and bowing to your partner as an embodiment of God—a reflection of Your Self.

This can be practiced alone, by looking at yourself in a mirror, with the same intent—to see God in yourself.

Realize that the love you feel is everywhere, in everyone, and is an expression of impersonal love, even though it feels personal—for you feel it in your own heart.[25] This is Christ Love.

---

[25] See *The Impersonal Life,* by Joseph Benner (Devorss & Co., 1941).

Chapter 14
Your Power to Create

Whatever comes after the words "I AM" is what you create. As you take responsibility for the I AM in you, you become a Master. Make sure, though, that what you want to create comes from Inner Guidance, and not just personal desire. This is not the law of attraction that has been heavily promoted, where you think you want a Ferrari, and then do affirmations to get one as soon as possible. First, ask God, "What do I need?" Get your ego and its desires out of the way. Then say and feel:

*I AM bringing into being
what God wants me to have,
which is coming to me in
perfect Divine Order.*

Every morning when I wake up I say:

*I AM the Great Divine Director
of this day.*

I AM God in action throughout the day.

The guidance will come from the subtle feeling in your heart. As you go about your day, check in with your heart and ask, "Does this feel good or not?" If it feels good, keep going in that direction—continue doing what you are doing. If it doesn't feel good, stop, tune in again, and say:

*I AM being shown where to go and
what to do, and I AM doing it.*

If you want to accelerate your Ascension, you can say and feel:

I AM the Ascension in the Light.

Your body is Consciousness vibrating according to your thoughts. You think you are somebody. You think you know who you are, that you are confined by your name, job, personality, and friends—but if you let go of those thoughts, you will be free. You can do whatever you want, but if you want to Ascend, bring more Light into every aspect of your life. Say and feel:

I AM the Light of God in action.

I AM the Resurrection and the Life.

I AM One with God right here and now.

Every time you say these words, you are raising your frequency and ascending. However, before you ask to completely ascend into your Higher Self, ask yourself, "Am I really ready to leave the Earth now?"

I have said "no" a number of times. If I had left, you wouldn't be reading this book. I feel as if I'm halfway between here and there, but I choose to be here—or relatively here—so I can interact with you on this plane. We can all help *light each other's fire,* as the '60s group, The Doors, sang in their famous song.

Any two of you can do this meditation together—even online. You can do this "looking meditation" with a friend or even in the mirror. See your image as the Presence of God and say, *I bless you.*

Or look in the mirror and say,

*I love you, God,
please reveal yourself to me.*

This is not done from the ego's point of view. Truly, your Real Self is a God that chose to be in this form at this time. You are a God who is choosing to learn something new here on Earth.

Ask God:

Please show me what I need to learn.

Then affirm:

*I AM learning what I need to learn
in Perfect, Divine Order.*

This is what Jesus meant when he said, *When two or more are gathered in my name, I AM there.* This special connection happens when people have their eyes open and see Christ in each other.

The essence of the Christ is to be in the world—helping other people. You can sit in the Light as long as you want, and it's beautiful—you can do as many affirmations as you want—but when you really want to share the Christ Light and Love with another person, it is important to have your eyes open.

A lot of my work is done with eyes open because then I release my activity into the human world. Sometimes I get up in the morning and turn around in a circle, hands outstretched, and say:

I AM the Presence of the Living God blessing humanity.

Or I turn in a circle as Violet Tara, saying:

I AM sending Violet Fire throughout the Earth.

Humanity needs your help, so say to

everyone on earth:

Feel this Light I AM sending out, for I AM the Presence of God blessing you, blessing humanity everywhere.

You affect everyone, no matter where your body is, because there is no space between thoughts. *Where your attention is, there you are,* as my teacher Pearl used to frequently say. Sitting in a room in Des Moines, Iowa, you can affect people in the African town of Timbuktu. This has been confirmed by people at a great distance, who have felt the energy I have sent.

There is an allegory: A long time ago, the Masters said that because humanity had made such a mess of things in past ages, they were going to hide the secret of power where people wouldn't find it for a long time—not until they were purified of all temptation for its misuse. "*We will hide the Secret in the last place they will think to look—in their own hearts.*"

I thought I had to go to the Himalayas to find this secret, but all I had to do was look within. I could even have looked in the mirror, like when I was a child—but at that time I didn't understand the light I was seeing. To understand and learn how to use this Light, I had to wait another twenty years—to find my teacher, Pearl.[26]

---

[26] See my biography: *Lady Master Pearl, My Teacher* (Church of the Seven Rays, 2014)

Chapter 15
What About the World?

Concerning the current state of the world, do not be seduced by the news, propaganda and discord. To understand what is going on, affirm:

There is nothing hidden that I need to know that is not revealed in perfect Divine Order!

I AM the illumining, revealing Presence, showing me the truth about this.

I AM being shown why this is happening and what the lesson is.

I AM being shown the inner workings of all that I need to know.

I AM being shown what to do, and I am doing it!

Then let go of all preconceptions, expectations, or anything you have read. The truth is beyond what most people comprehend—and definitely beyond what is in the news. Ask your God Presence:

What can I do?

Perhaps it is just to be still, meditate, and send out love. The great *mahasiddhas* (highly realized beings) and saints around the world, living in the mountains or even in cities, may find their role is to just pour out unconditional Love and Illumination to the world—expanding their own consciousness to embrace that of humanity. Sometimes that is the best thing we can do. Those great beings act out of the absolute Divine necessity and inner guidance of God, not out of any personal desire or emotion. Once again, to master yourself, master your attention. Do not be drawn into dwelling on all the theories that make you think that you know the truth about who should do what.

What is our purpose? We are here to learn compassion for all beings, to help them grow into their Divinity.

Someone once asked the great Indian yogi, Ramana Maharshi (1879-1950), who spent most of his life on Mount Arunachala in Southern India, "What good are you doing sitting on this mountain? Don't you think you should go out into the world and help others?"

He replied: *What others?*

In his state of consciousness, all others were a part of himself. He affected humanity, as we all do, through *just being.*

Chapter 16
Other Meditations

It doesn't matter what path you follow, you can always still your mind. Using *shamatha* meditation, just feel the rise and fall of your chest. Feel the in-breath and out-breath. If your mind goes to something, to some idea, feeling, or sensation, label the distraction as "thinking," then come back to the in-breath and the out-breath. Gradually, your mind relaxes, and you start to feel a sense of peace and stillness. You find that between your thoughts there's empty space in which there is the experience of Oneness with All. Let your consciousness expand without limit. Next, you can introduce *vipassana* practice and ask, "Who is experiencing this?" More correctly, it is not *who* but *What?* Identify with *That.* In Sanskrit, it is said: *Tat Twam Asi,* meaning "You are That!"

Or you can do the light meditation that Saint Germain gives in *Unveiled Mysteries.* Imagine a great light in the center of your being. Your body is translucent, and in its center is a *sun*. Its sunlight is filling every part of your body and radiating out into space. Keep expanding and intensifying that light. Say and feel:

I AM the Light of God.

Sense the nearness of the Presence—It feels like Love. That is God's Love within you. Say and feel:

I AM the Light of God radiating out to all. I love the Light. I serve the Light. I live in the Light. I AM the Light.

When you realize the true nature of Reality, you see things anew. The change that is required is to change our perceptions. From the beginning of time, I AM has been known as the secret way to invoke God—the True Self—and to become a worker of miracles. The joke is that we think this world is the ultimate reality, when actually it is only our dream, whose purpose is to teach us to love.

Chapter 17
Methods of Meditation[27]

1) ***Vipassana:*** Sit cross-legged or in a chair, with spine straight, chin slightly lowered, eyes partially closed and looking downward. If sitting in a chair, feet should be flat on the ground. Hands rest on knees or in the lap with one palm resting in the other. The tip of the tongue is against the roof of the mouth (to complete the bio-electric circuit). Observe the inbreath and outbreath, allowing the attention to rest in the center of the chest. When a thought arises, label it *thinking* and come back to the breath. This leads to a state of calmness known in Sanskrit as *Shamatha*.

Next, inquire into the nature of the Self:

What is observing the mind?

Some teachings say to ask *Who,* but this can lead back to the ego, so I suggest

---

[27] These meditations go by other names in various traditions.

asking *What* is observing. This leads into immersion in the sea of unlimited Awareness.

This two-part practice is the one used by Siddhartha Gautama to awaken as the Buddha, the *one who is awake.*

2) ***Self Inquiry:*** While engaging in the calming shamatha practice above, you can also examine your egoic self, the thoughts, feeling, and emotions, that almost constantly pass through your awareness, and that need purification. This is a form of self-therapy that can heal deep-seated emotional issues.

Ask:

What am I feeling?

How did that feeling arise?

When is the last time I felt that?

When is the first time I experienced that?

Have I caused anyone else to feel that, either in this or a past life?

Is having that feeling serving me?

*Can I now let go of that feeling
and feel equanimity?*

*I now feel the fullness of the
Presence of God within myself.*

*I Am healing myself, and others,
who are also myself.*

You may also invoke the Violet Consuming Flame to dissolve any energetic residue, followed by the Sword of Blue Flame of Archangel Michael, to free you from all negativity forever.

3) ***Mindfulness:*** This is meditation in action. It is the logical outcome of the above methods of meditation carried over into daily life. A method that helps sustain the consciousness of Oneness is to first be aware of the True Self residing in the heart, then be aware of the True Self residing in the other person, then hold the

awareness of the I AM Presence, God, overhead as the Observer. Holding these three points of awareness simultaneously enables one to act consciously while still residing in Oneness. Or simply be fully conscious, with an open heart, in whatever situation you find yourself.

Tibetan meditation master Chögyam Trungpa Rinpoche writes this beautifully below. What he calls the Great Eastern Sun is the teaching of basic goodness and *Samsara* is the illusion that conventional life will make you happy.[28]

Hold the sadness and pain of samsara in your heart and at the same time the power and vision of the Great Eastern Sun. Then the warrior can make a proper cup of tea.

---

[28] Basic goodness is the realization that our true nature is good, even in those who do bad things. This is the opposite of the Christian doctrine, introduced by Saint Augustine, that we are born sinners, a teaching not found in the words of Jesus.

In other words, you are fully aware of the suffering in the world and the goodness in your own heart—while at the same time being in conscious action.

Attaining this mindfulness can be brought about through the methods given here. Tibetan lamas, including the Dalai Lama, are frequently seen using their bead malas to recite mantras, even while walking or being interviewed. This is to keep their minds anchored in the present moment, free of extraneous thoughts and emotions.

In Buddhism there is also the Pure Land teaching, which does not require formal sitting practice, where you see all phenomena as the body, speech, mind, and heart of the Buddha. When you go for a walk you see the grass as the hair of the Buddha (or the Divine Mother, who is also a Buddha), the leaves on the trees as the hands of the Buddha, all people you encounter as living Buddhas, all words exchanged as the words of a Buddha, all thoughts you perceive as thoughts of the Buddha, and all that you feel as the heart of the Buddha. Basically, everything is perceived as the Buddha, which expands you out of duality into the world beyond ego, where nothing is taken personally.[29]

4) **Tantra**: also called *Vajrayana*, often translated in Sanskrit as thunderbolt teachings, recognizes that everything exists as part of a web of unbroken awareness, the consciousness of which can be realized by seeing external phenomena as an aspect of Oneself. This method employs *mantra*, or an affirmation, repeated in one's native language; *mudra,* a gesture or movement; and visualization. The first phase (generation phase) is to visualize a

---

[29] The Pure Land Teaching traditionally mentions only the body, speech, and mind aspects of the Buddha; however, to transcend the historical patriarchal tendency of Buddhism, we must also include the heart and the feeling aspect of awareness.

particular Deity or Ascended Master in front of one. Make the being more and more real. See the being turn into Light and merge with you. Then you become the Being (completion phase) and enact the activity of that particular Deity. For example, if you invoke Archangel Michael, you feel yourself become Him in action in a particular situation, then take His Sword of Blue Flame in your hand and use it to liberate people and conditions, saying at the same time:

I AM Archangel Michael in action here, freeing all beings from limitation forever.

Lastly, you return the sword to Archangel Michael and see him either depart or continue to reside above the situation or even above you. However, you return to your normal state of relative awareness as separate from the Deity. This practice can also be done with *yidams,* meditational Deities who have never embodied on earth as humans, but who represent aspects of consciousness that can be invoked to act as real beings. This method is explained in greater detail in my two books on Violet Tara.

The use of I AM Affirmations as given in the Saint Germain teachings, if done properly, is actually a tantric practice. Otherwise, if done solely from the mind and speech, is simply an exercise of human will. To be truly effective, affirmations must be done from the inner Consciousness, free of ego, which can only be achieved through meditation.

5) ***Inner Light Meditation:*** While seated, still your mind by observing your breath. Turn your attention inward to the center of your being, which can be felt in the center of your chest. This is where the Sacred Flame from the I AM Presence, which keeps you alive, is anchored in your physical body. As you dwell on this Light *(jyoti)* within you, gradually begin to feel a pleasant sensation of love. Visualize a sphere of Light in the center of your chest. Gradually expand that Light to become a sun whose rays extend outward. Know

that your body is not solid, but a focus of thought and energy vibrating at a certain frequency, which becomes translucent. As the sun within you expands, that Inner Light shines outward and through you into the room. Your body becomes Light. Expand that Light even more and watch the sunlight of your being fill the world and all Creation. Say and feel:

*I AM the Living Light.
I AM the Sun of God
illumining the World.*

A similar Light meditation is given by Saint Germain in the first chapter of *Unveiled Mysteries* (Godfre Ray King, Saint Germain Press).

6) ***Sun Meditation:*** This incorporates both tantric meditation as well as the above Light meditation. An ideal time to practice is right after sunrise or just before sunset. Otherwise, this meditation should be done either with eyes closed or gazing downward. Without staring at the Sun,

which would damage the eyes, be aware of the Sun as a focal point of God Consciousness, knowing that there is an etheric Sun that co-exists with the physical Sun, inhabited by God Beings who shine the Light of their Consciousness on the Earth. So called "primitive" societies who practiced Sun worship knew this. The goal is not to worship the physical orb but to see it as a reflection of one's own Higher Self, the I AM Presence made visible above you. As you send Love from your heart to the Sun, you may say and feel:

I love you and give thanks to you for sustaining life on Earth. I ask for your Consciousness to permeate mine so that I, too, become a Sun radiating Love, Light and Healing to humanity.

You may also say the Gayatri Mantra, which is a powerful Sanskrit invocation of Gayatri, the Goddess of Light, to make your mind, body, and soul, one with the Cosmic Light. See and feel your mind, body, and soul fill with Light as you say:

Om Bhūḥ Bhuvaḥ Suvaha,
Tat Savitur Varenyam,
Bhargo Devasya Dhīmahi,
Dhiyo Yo Naḥ Pracodāyat.

7) **Mantra Meditation:** The Sanskrit word *mantra* is made up of two roots: *man* (mind) and *tra* (protect), so a mantra is that which protects the mind. Sanskrit is a primordial language predating the existence of earthly humanity. The above Gayatri Mantra, according to Sathya Sai Baba, existed prior to the Earth. The sounds composing Sanskrit activate the spiritual centers *(chakras)* as well as the subtle nervous system *(nadis)*. Sanskrit has been used from the beginning of time, not only to foster personal evolution and health, but to regenerate creation. Mantras should be recited daily for the prescribed number of times. It helps you to focus, as well as to keep track of the number of repetitions, if you obtain a *mala*, which is a string containing 108 beads.

It is good to start the learning process by repeating the mantra aloud, but it becomes more powerful when done silently. In fact, the Tibetans say that every mantra can be recited four different ways: outer, inner, secret, and hidden, methods which cannot be explained verbally.

There are certain well-known and powerful mantras, such as the Gayatri above, or the Tara mantra below, that can be used with great benefit:

Om Tare Tuttare Ture Swaha.

There is also the Vajra Guru Mantra given specifically for the present time by Padmasambhava:

Om Ah Hung
Vajra Guru
Padma Siddhi Hung

The first three words represent the 3rd eye center of consciousness, the speech center, and the heart center. The Vajra Guru is your I AM Presence manifesting as the indestructible teacher who is everywhere and in everything. The Padma is the lotus of the Divine Mother who is always enfolding you in Her embrace. Siddhi Hung affirms your attainment of the full power and accomplishment of this mantra.

The Chenrezig Mantra is for the generation of compassion:

Om Mani Padme Hum

More specific mantras can be obtained from the rare, enlightened being; or heard in meditation in response to your request for a mantra; or from a competent Vedic astrologer. The one or two-word mantras marketed to the public by organizations, although they may aid in learning concentration, do not have much long-term spiritual benefit. When you do obtain a personal mantra, do not reveal it or discuss it with others, as this depletes the accumulated energy attained by your practice.

On the most basic level the repetition of a mantra helps still the mind, resulting in a calmness that allows one to tune in to the primordial Self, which facilitates enlightenment. On another level, the vibrations of Sanskrit purify the lower self as well as the environment. The mantra, being repeated during the visualization of the Deity, is an intrinsic part of the tantric practice. In fact, the sound frequencies facilitate the completion phase during which you become one with the Deity.

8) ***Love Meditation:*** We always hear, *Love yourself,* but how? Most people interpret that as to love and honor the human self, the ego-based personality. People were instructed to think of good things they had done, good aspects of their personality, and feel pride in themselves. However, that is only the illusory self, and paying respects to that self only increases pride, vanity, and attachment to ego. Love of the Real Self is something entirely

different, and leads to not only greater Love of God, the Higher Self, but greater love for humanity.

Imagine yourself when you were a baby, perhaps three months old. You were held by someone who loved you very much—probably your mother, but also possibly an aunt, cousin, or sibling. That person is holding you in their arms and looking at you with great tenderness, love, and compassion. Switch now to the image of that person being you—holding your infant self in your arms. Look down on that helpless, tender, lovable baby, and say:

I love you. I will always love you. You are without blame and totally good. You are going to go through many challenges in this life but know that I will always love you and be here for you.

Feel your heart expand. Your infant self feels the love too, and it becomes more and more a being of light as it merges with your heart. Gradually, your infant self becomes one with your Inner Light. You can say and feel:

I AM Love. I AM Light. I AM wholly pure and perfect.

See the Light in your heart expand. Your body becomes translucent like crystal as the Light fills your body and radiates out into space. This ball of white and golden Light becomes enveloped in the pink Light of Divine Love as it continues to expand outward. Say and feel:

I AM Divine Love radiating out to humanity. My Love is God's Love. God's Love is filling the World, and I AM That Love!

Know that a similar infant is in everyone, so when you think of or talk to others, be aware of that child that has been hurt, that needs your love and understanding. Send Love from your heart to that child residing in the hearts of all beings.

9) *Tonglen:* Compassion

This combines several of the above methods and shifts the focus somewhat from self-enlightenment to enlightenment for all. Instead of seeing suffering as "out there," and that people need to be "saved," realize that the others are aspects of yourself. Meditating on their suffering becomes a means to alleviate your own suffering, and to expand your own love and compassion.

First, be aware of your breathing, the in-breath and the out-breath, until you become calm and serene. Then, feel the Light in the center of your chest, which you may feel more as Love, or simply Energy.

You don't want to take on the suffering of others, for then there would be more suffering. You are going to transmute the condition. Do this by feeling and sending out love. Imagine the suffering is like a fog. There's a sort of heaviness to it, which you are aware of as you breathe in—and then you exhale the lightness of Light, Love, and Joy.

With the inhalation you are aware of the heaviness, and with the exhalation you feel your lightness going out into the world, filling the hearts, minds, and souls of all beings with Love and Joy.

You become a tremendous blessing to humanity as well as yourself. What you send out is what you receive. What you think is what you are. Thus, it is better to think Love and Joy. Think and feel:

I Am a transmitter of Light, Love and Joy, filling my heart, body, room, home, community, country, and the entire Earth.

Imagine you are in your etheric body that is made of Light, Your heart is a great expanding sun. Rays of Love and Compassion are flooding forth from your heart into the world, and the Earth also becomes a Sun. You say and feel:

I Am a Sun of God filling humanity with

Light, Love, and Happiness.

I Am the Violet Consuming Flame, blazing forth throughout the Earth, dissolving and consuming anything less than perfection.

I Am grateful to my Ascended older brothers and sisters: Mother Mary, Mary Magdalene, Quan Yin, El Morya, Kuthumi, Paul the Venetian, Serapis Bey, Hilarion, Jesus, Saint Germain, Lord Maha Chohan, Great Divine Director, Mighty Victory, Sanat Kumara, and all Angels, Archangels and Cosmic Beings. Above all, I Am grateful to my God Presence, without which my heart would not beat. Thank you, beloved God Presence, for keeping me alive in this body—healthy and functioning—so I may fulfill my mission on Earth.

In this way you become God in Action at your point in space and time, evolving yourself as you help humanity in its evolution.

You have a divine mission. If you don't know what that is, say:

*I Am the resurrection and the life
of my divine mission on earth
now made fully manifest.*

That mission may manifest very humbly. It could be simply meditating. It doesn't have to be going out into the streets like Mother Theresa and taking care of the homeless, although it could be that too. Just being, transmuting the negative into positive, is an amazing and fantastic mission. Even just feel:

I Am Love.

10) ***Spontaneous Awareness:*** This is not a method but a state of consciousness where there is no awareness of your human self, personality, surroundings, or the world. You merge into a state of *satchitananda,* loosely translated as being, consciousness, and bliss. However, these words are inadequate to describe what is beyond human reality—perceivable only after relative consciousness has begun to return. This state can be achieved in different ways, usually only after learning to still the mind and inquiring into the nature of the Self. However, on rare occasions, samadhi can also manifest spontaneously through Divine Grace. It also has various levels of absorption.

This is a meditation without support, as you enter the state of awareness spontaneously and at will without using any method. Some of the previous methods are meditations with support, that use various techniques, such as a mantra or observation of the breath, to launch one into higher consciousness.

This realization of Oneness with the Absolute is the foundation of Advaita Vedanta. You are aware that you are an eternal soul, *atman,* that is one with God, *Brahman,* yet are also aware that you are in the world—which you perceive as an illusion, which can not affect you. As stated in Sanskrit: *Tat Twam Asi*. This is the path so clearly enunciated by the Indian sage, Ramana Maharshi. It is also the fruition of Zen and Tibetan Dzogchen practice *(Maha Atti),* where it is known as meditation without meditating.

Chapter 18
Concise Method of Liberation
Inspired by Padmasambhava,
July 11, 2021

The great enlightened master in eighth century Tibet, Padmasambhava, foresaw the decadent condition of our present age, including the invasion of Tibet, and said *When the iron bird flies and horses run on wheels the Dharma will go to the land of the red man* (Native Americans). The method I give here was inspired by Padmasambhava to make that Buddhist Dharma further accessible to Western spiritual aspirants—for this present time of confusion requires clear, concise instruction to realize our true nature. The following practice is self-liberating and contains the foundation of Buddhist teachings: the *Ngondro prayer* (preliminary practice), the *Four Thoughts that Turn the Mind to the Dharma,* and the

Four Noble Truths (including the *Eight-Fold Path.*)

Think inwardly and feel:

> *I prostrate to the Buddha, the Dharma, and the Sangha.*

In the West, we are trained to not bow to anyone, yet bowing to God is not the same as bowing to a person or ruler and is a powerful way to subdue your ego. Try prostrating flat out on the floor, hands stretched overhead, offering yourself to the Living God, and you will be amazed at how good this feels. You are offering your confused lower self to your all-knowing Higher Self, God, which Buddhists call your Dharmakaya or Buddha nature. You are also vowing to follow the Dharma, the path to liberation, as the guiding principle of your life. Lastly, you are joining with the Sangha, which is the community of your fellow aspirants and all enlightened beings who have followed the path to Buddhahood.

Raise your hands above your head in prayer, then bring your clasped hands down to touch your brow, mouth, and heart, representing enlightened body, speech, and mind. Bend forward and stretch out with face down on the floor and hands reaching forward to the feet of the Buddha, (your Higher Self) who you imagine standing before you. Imagine your family and friends on either side of you. See your enemies, or those you feel threatened by or feel distant from, standing in front of you, also facing the Buddha, repeating the same practice. This helps not only liberate others but frees you from any attachment to them.[30]

As you stretch out face down, hands over your head, say silently:

---

[30] There are several good YouTube videos showing how to do a full prostration.

I take refuge in the Buddha (God, your I AM Presence) and implore your unceasing guidance until I attain full enlightenment and Mastery. (Refuge does not mean hiding, but seeking guidance, instruction, as well as protection.)

As you stand up, think:

Until samsara ends, I will bring about benefit all beings by my thoughts, words, and actions.

After your prostrations, sit and meditate. Feel:

I am grateful for this precious life that allows me to experience myself as a Buddha.

Meditate on the truth of karma, that all thoughts and energy travel in a circle and return to the sender. These are the causes that have brought you to your present place in life:

I know that my experiences in this life are the outcome of my own previous choices in past lives or earlier in this life—so I cease to see experiences as good or bad—but as lessons moving me toward Mastery and liberation from the world of illusion.

Contemplate the Four Noble Truths:

I do not expect lasting happiness to come from the ever-changing world of illusion.

I let go of all attachment to attaining certain results in the world of illusion and instead focus on what is eternal.

I am grateful to have found the path to liberation from suffering.

I will now walk that Path of the Enlightened Ones who have gone before me. I will strive diligently on this Eight-Fold Path to:

1) Understand the nature of reality.
2) Cease to hold limiting thoughts about myself and others.
3) Speak the truth, not talk excessively, and use only words that cause benefit.
4) Act only in ways that cause benefit.
5) Exert diligent effort to achieve these goals.
6) Pursue a livelihood and path in life that benefits others without causing harm.
7) Observe my thoughts and emotions, realizing that I am separate from them.
8) Meditate on awareness—and become one with that awareness.

These eight precepts contain the essence of the path to liberation from the most basic, of not causing harm, to the most advanced—unlimited awareness. Numbers 7 and 8 constitute two basic types of meditation that are a core practice.

I implore all enlightened beings who have gone before me to be aware of me this moment. Help me follow this path and achieve these objectives so I may attain liberation and so benefit all beings.

Afterword

So, what path should I follow?

I would propose the Middle Path, the path between two seemingly opposite practices, the pursuit of blissful Oneness on one hand, and the observation of mindfulness of the present moment on the other. This does not mean to exclude either path, for they each offer many blessings—and in the end, they both merge in the attainment of full Mastery.

The trick, however, is to not go to the extreme of making either path the ultimate reality. On the one hand, the awareness of the ego disappears, and you experience God Consciousness, but you cannot function in the world, drive a car, hold a job, or be in relationship—for no "one" is *there.* On the other hand, you are completely grounded in the present moment, able to function in day-to-day life, but possibly out of touch with the love and joy of the Source. On the path of true

Mastery both extremes merge in God Conscious Action.

The concept of this middle path came from the experience of the one we call Buddha, the Awakened One, during his time as a wandering ascetic. As he sat on the bank of a river, he saw a boat going upstream. In it was a musician tuning a sitar. The ascetic realized that if the musician left the string slack it would not make any sound, but if he tightened it too much the string would snap. He saw this as a reflection of his own predicament. If he was a glutton and indulged his senses, his mind would become dull, but if he was too ascetic he would not have the energy to cut through illusion and achieve liberation. He realized that by being moderate in his diet and spiritual practices, following a middle path, he would be more likely to succeed. At that moment, the story goes, a passing girl saw the gaunt figure of the ascetic and was inspired to offer him the sweetened milk she was carrying home from the market. As he drank the offering, he became energized and saw the true nature of his Mind—free of all concepts—attaining full Enlightenment.

Each of us is in the process of becoming a Buddha, as we awaken to our True Nature from the dream of duality. What keeps us asleep is our clinging to ego, its desires, and concepts. And why do we cling? Perhaps because clinging to the dream we know seems safer and more comfortable than to awaken to the complete freedom of a totally new reality—like zoo animals that sometimes become shocked or confused when suddenly freed from their cages.

Then which path should we follow? The ego finds it easier to believe that one path is true, and another path is false. The same extreme ideas exist in all walks of life from religion to politics. It is much easier to cling to a concept, holding to the certainty that one is right, rather than to live in open uncommitted awareness, accepting the validity of many possibilities, but clinging to none—for ultimate Truth cannot be found in any one path, only within Yourself.

As you awaken as a Buddha, you become aware of the God Presence that exists within and in the higher octaves above you, while at the same time being aware of your surroundings and those you are in relationship with at the present moment. In that awareness, call forth your I AM Presence and be the Master of your world.

One who is asleep does not know the sleeper. Yet as the One awakens It becomes aware of Itself, expressing Its joy as OM. Further awake, It realizes Itself as I, then desires to manifest as AM. Thus, duality is born, and a self that creates experience, cause and effect with its various lessons. Once learned, the Soul returns again to the Source, knowing Itself as Being...Consciousness... and Bliss.

-Peter Mt. Shasta

*Don't mistake mere words to be
the meaning of the teachings.
Mingle the practice with your own
being and attain liberation
from samsara right now!*

-Padmasambhava

Peter Mt. Shasta

Other Books by Peter Mt. Shasta

"I AM" the Open Door

"I AM" Affirmations and the Secret of their Effective Use

"I AM" The Living Christ

"I AM" the Violet Tara

*I AM Violet Tara in Action,
Lessons in Mastery*

*Search for the Guru:
Adventures of a Western Mystic, Book I*

*Apprentice to the Masters:
Adventures of a Western Mystic: Book II*

*My Search in Tibet for the Secret
Wish-Fulfilling Jewel*

Lady Master Pearl, My Teacher

Step By Step, Ascended Master Discourses

It Is What It Is

The 16th Karmapa merging with his Rainbow Body as he invokes the Buddha of Infinite Compassion prior to performing the Black Crown ceremony in San Francisco around 1970.

Printed in Dunstable, United Kingdom